MAKE
FRIENDS WITH
Your
Shadow

*How to Accept
and Use Positively
the Negative Side of
Your Personality*

WILLIAM A. MILLER

AUGSBURG Publishing House • Minneapolis

MAKE FRIENDS WITH YOUR SHADOW

Copyright © 1981 William A. Miller

Library of Congress Catalog Card No. 80-67793

International Standard Book No. 0-8066-1855-8

Scripture quotations unless otherwise noted are from the Re-
vised Standard Version of the Bible, copyright 1946, 1952, and
1971 by the Division of Christian Education of the National
Council of Churches.

The Scripture quotation marked JB is from the Jerusalem
Bible, copyright 1966 by Doubleday & Company, Inc.

MANUFACTURED IN THE UNITED STATES OF AMERICA

To

the memory of my

Aunt Olga and Uncle Lou

Contents

Introduction

I very much like a story which Joseph Sittler enjoys telling on himself and a certain Dr. Platz. For many years Dr. Sittler was a professor of theology at the University of Chicago Divinity School. He reveals how each school day at noon a white truck marked "Hot Dogs, Polish Sausage, Coffee" would park in front of the administration building and dispense its goodies.

"The main item," says Sittler, "was the Polish sausage sandwich. This particular sandwich was no ordinary product! Rich, juicy, odorous, garlic-laden, hot, and smelling with all the herb-subtlety of a thousand years of Polish sausage culture, this creation would be lifted out of a steaming hot container, laid in an oblong bun, and garnished with chopped onions, mustard, pickle relish, and green peppers. It had a shocking authority and pungency, bringing tears to the eyes, a clutch at the throat, and clarification to the mind!"

One day when Dr. Sittler joined the line to indulge himself in one of these gastronome's delights, he was astonished to see a friend directly in front of him.

"Dr. Platz," he exclaimed, "what are you doing here? You are a pathologist. You know very well that you ought not to eat one of those violent things! Now I am only a theologian and don't know any better. But *you* are a doctor, a pathologist at that—and you have professionally excised the catastrophic

9

effect upon the stomach of these explosive, corrosive, tissue-eroding sausages! Those fiery peppers, to mention but one component of this symphony, are enough in themselves to make the white cells cry out in anguish!"

Charles Platz simply fixed on Dr. Sittler with a cool gaze and said quietly, "Yes, of course, you are quite right. But these things *are* very good, aren't they?"

So Dr. Sittler and Dr. Platz went right on doing what they knew full well they shouldn't.

In his delightful humor, Joseph Sittler confesses his perversity. In a more tragic way a headline declares the same trait: Some Smokers Still Ignore the Evidence. A 1980 study of the mortality of adult smokers versus nonsmokers revealed a significant difference in favor of nonsmokers. That fact was recognized by 50 United States life insurance firms who offered rate discounts to nonsmokers. Nevertheless . . .

The Apostle Paul of nearly 20 centuries ago had, I would suppose, neither Polish sausage nor tobacco to bewitch him, but his perversity was just as real, if not more so. "The good that I would I do not," he cried out, "but the evil which I would not, that I do" (Rom 7:19 KJV).

"Knowing better" seems to make little impact on perversity. Martin Luther lamented: "We still have much frailty and sin on our necks. . . . And we feel so many evil lusts after Baptism because we have to fight and wrestle with the flesh! God could justly condemn and punish this sin; for much of the old Adam still creeps into our actions. There is no denying this."

Yet many would deny it. Many of us want desperately to deny our perversity and pretend it isn't there. We believe that it will somehow vanish or dissolve if we bury it or drown it or crucify it.

In my book *Why Do Christians Break Down?* (Augsburg,

1973), I explored various aspects of the relationship of religion to mental health. The book examined the possibility that the organized, structured, traditional Christian church might in some of its emphases be actually contributing to emotional breakdown in the lives of some of the people it touches. One chapter was titled, "The Shadow." It asked, "Why do I break down?", and answered, "I break down because I am afraid to admit that evil, unacceptable, inappropriate tendencies still exist within me, even though I have committed myself to the way of Christ, and I cannot accept them as being truly a part of me."

The positive interest in the shadow which that brief introduction to it raised prompted me to set out on the task of creating a more comprehensive presentation of this fascinating subject. That was in 1974; this volume is the result.

Carl Gustav Jung, son of a clergyman and one of the three founders of modern psychiatry, is largely responsible for the concept of the shadow, and it is to him and his writings that this work is indebted. Literally hundreds of people who have written about Jung's psychology have also provided me with material and insight. Likewise my own professional experiences and my own shadow have offered invaluable assistance. The subject definitely has its technical and complicated aspects, but I have endeavored to keep the text of the book simple and conversational.

Throughout much of the modern church such stress has been placed on the development of goodness and righteousness *per se* that even the mere mention among Christian people of that which is dark and shadowy often seems out of place. The suggestion that it be befriended may be considered even more radical. Still it is my observation that substantially more harm is done by denying and repressing the shadow than by coming to grips with it. Those who deny their shadows only project their evil onto others and see it in them. Those who repress their shadows to maintain their purity and innocence are sometimes overcome by them and swept away in their very own evil.

Jesus and Paul appear in Scripture to have taken differing views of what to do with the shadow, Paul seeming to encourage repression of it, and Jesus seeming to encourage befriending it. Why the church has apparently followed Paul's approach more than that of Jesus may very well be because coming to grips with and befriending the shadow requires substantial moral courage; it is demanding and risky, but rewarding.

The thesis of this book may be stated thus: Movement towards the achievement of wholeness or completeness (or "perfection" in the sense of Jesus' use of the Greek word *teleios*) is accomplished *not only* through the continued infusion of goodness, righteousness, and morality (striving after the good), *but also* through the acceptance (the "owning") and conscious incorporation of one's dark and shadowy side into one's self. I am not a complete person until I incorporate into my conscious self that dark side of my person which is every bit as much a part of me as is that bright self which I parade before the world.

We are to fight evil, but we are to learn from it. We resist it, but we use it for good. We are to take that which may appear to be undesirable, unacceptable, and even objectionable and use it positively, constructively, and even creatively, thus bringing ourselves closer towards wholeness and completion. This, in fact, is our task!

"Remember," said Jesus, "I am sending you out like sheep among wolves; so be cunning as serpents and yet harmless as doves" (Matt. 10:16 JB).

Make friends with your shadow!

12

1

SHADOW

and personality development

What a way to begin! At birth we are not even aware that there is a distinction between our selves and anything else. As far as we are concerned, all is one and all is "I." For instance, an infant appears to have no realization that at some clearly definable point in space his lips end and his mother's nipple or the nursing bottle begins. In his awareness, there is no distinction— they are one and the same. He has no cognizance of the fact that a great gulf separates the gnawing emptiness in his stomach and the source of nourishment and satisfaction in his mother's breast or the nursing bottle. He believes his cries enable him to feed himself.

Ah, to believe that you and the cosmos are one is indeed a very desirable position to hold. It is also a relatively reasonable one for infants: they believe they are omnipotent, and any parent can attest to the power and control exercised by seven and one-half pounds of newborn humanity. The fact that infants are successful in their omnipotence and egocentricity explains their survival. If they didn't get their way by manipulating their environment at two in the morning, they would never make it.

With the experience of such successful egomania fresh at hand, it is not at all difficult to realize that the first and probably greatest lesson of life is one of the hardest; namely that "I" and the "Not-I" exist—that "I" and the universe are separate entities and are not commingled into one; and that furthermore "I" must make an approach to "Not-I" or "That-other" if "That-other" is to supply my wants and meet my needs which I myself cannot.

The fact that we are "egomaniacs," firmly believing in our egocentricity in our infancy, is good. But one of the major tasks of life is to lay aside, piece by piece, the egocentricity that is natural to our infancy, and to accept the hard truth that we cannot everlastingly have our own way. Most people do a relatively decent job of this task over their lifetime; some people struggle with it, periodically rebelling and regressing to their infant expectations; a few never really abandon their egomania at all, but go to their graves still firmly fixed in the belief that the universe does indeed orbit around them.

Just when the differentiation between "I" and "Not-I" begins in the life of the infant cannot be pinpointed. But judging from behaviors it is quite early indeed that "I" realize (certainly on a primitive level) that "I" must *relate* to "That-other"—the outer world. Here we are confronted with the two realms of human experience: the outer world and the inner world. The outer world is the tangible, the concrete, the world of matter and substance, all that comes to us through our bodily senses, all that is here and now in space and time. The inner world is the realm of nonmaterial phenomena, the unconscious, the spiritual, that which is perceived as extrasensory. In psychological terms it is the human psyche which serves as a sort of channel connecting these two worlds and relating to both.

Because the outer world is where the needs and wants of infancy are met it is at that end of the channel that the developing child will focus his psychic energy and attention; the other end, the inner world, will usually remain neglected and unattended until later in life.

It isn't long before the infant learns that some forms of relating and patterns of behavior are more productive of rewards than others. The infant may realize, for instance, that a smile and a burp will usually earn soft, soothing sounds from the mouth of "That-other" and probably even the comfort, warmth, and security of being held closely. On the other hand he will learn that urinating on the wall while his diaper is being changed will usually merit harsh, loud sounds from the mouth of "That-other" and possibly even the sensation of stinging pain in his buttocks. Consequently most infants, in their process of development, learn to present to "That-other" (the outer world) those qualities which it perceives "That-other" most likes to see in it and most adequately rewards.

Thus it is that parents often speak of their little children ("the darlings") developing their own personalities very early in their young lives. Each child's personality development is unique and may, for instance, be quite different from the personalities of siblings; so much so sometimes that parents wonder if there wasn't a mistake made in the hospital and they have some other couple's child.

Whatever qualities or characteristics emerge in the personality, they seem to arise out of an unlimited possibility of traits resident in the psyche. It would appear that the human psyche by nature contains *in potential* all possible human traits or characteristics of personality. Furthermore it appears there is a law of psychic balance whereby when one quality is drawn into the end of the psyche which relates to the outer world, its opposite quality is dropped back to the other end of the psyche which is

15

closer to the inner world. For example, if a child finds in his environment that it is to his advantage to develop the qualities of submissiveness, obedience, quietness, and docility, then the opposite qualities of rebelliousness, stubbornness, and independence will be tucked away at the inner world end of the psyche (or down in the cellar, as I prefer to call it) and perhaps one day will quite unexpectedly come breaking through to the outer world (or bounding up those cellar stairs) and surprise everyone, the person himself included.

The characteristics of personality which are publicly displayed have the benefit of discipline and refinement through use; they get their corners and sharp edges rubbed off, so to speak, through constant relationship and interaction with the outer world and its criticism of them. The qualities dropped into the cellar at the inner world end of the psyche have no such advantages. They remain as crude and primitive as were *all* the qualities the child possessed. If any of these qualities should happen to make its way up to the personality presented to the outer world, it will inevitably create an unpleasant impression, because it will have the same unsophisticated, uncivilized character as did the baby's first kickings and screamings—amusing and forgivable in the infant, but unexpected and generally unacceptable, if not disgusting, in the older child or adult.

If it is true that all possible qualities lie in potential in the human psyche, what determines which qualities will be drawn into that personality which will relate to the outer world? Is it an arbitrary law of chance? Or the inevitability of genetic influence? Or the influence of the environment in which the child is developing?

In all likelihood it isn't the first. The second possibility cannot be discounted. But the third—environment—appears to be the greatest, most influential factor.

A child's parents generally are the most influential part of his environment. Children do not always develop the qualities their parents believe they would like them to develop, but they invariably develop the qualities which the parents evoke. Unfortunately most of this occurs on an unconscious level and parents never realize it is happening. Most parents know that children learn more by example than by precept, but not all parents realize their example as perceived by their child may not be what they intend it to be. For instance, a woman who is resigned to a position in life which she unconsciously detests may help develop a rebellious child simply because she has never faced and dealt with her own unconscious rebellion. The rebelliousness in the child is just as much evoked by the mother as if she had diligently taught it by words. Children learn far less from words and far more from emotional states which surround them, even if those emotional states are unknown to the parents (adults) generating them.

After having two children, Helen and Doug Hershey decided they would have one more child to complete their family. Helen became pregnant and at her time of delivery was somewhat startled to learn that she had had twin girls. There had been no indication of this during her pregnancy and she was mildly shocked by the news. But she seemed to recover quickly and indeed rejoiced over the two darling baby girls she and Doug took home from the hospital.

As the twin girls grew and developed, the differences in their personalities became increasingly obvious. Lois, the firstborn of the twins, was a gregarious, smiling, chatty youngster. Lola, the secondborn, was reserved, quiet, and appeared downcast, even melancholy. In time Helen decided to seek counseling for Lola because she feared for the child's emotional health. In the process of family therapy, Helen became aware of feelings with-

17

in herself which had been unconscious since the day she delivered the twins. She realized how much she had resented that second baby because of the disrupting effect she would have on the family. They had planned for only one more child, not two. Helen resented the extra work, the extra expense, and the far-reaching ramifications of this unexpected child. But guilt overwhelmed her and she put such thoughts out of her head and such feelings out of her being. Instead she rejoiced over the healthy and beautiful babies with which she had been blessed.

But those original feelings of resentment towards her second-born twin daughter had not been successfully dispelled; they had only been denied and repressed—pushed down into her unconscious. The little girl, with her sharp perception and clear sensitivity, picked up a message her mother didn't even know she was sending. Feeling the unconscious rejection from her mother, she began to reject herself. Even though the whole family honestly believed that Mom showed the same "face" to Lois and Lola alike, the unconscious difference in feeling towards the two girls got through to Lola and strongly influenced the development of her personality.

Certainly we cannot ignore the inherited, genetic influence on a child's personality development, but that influence compared to the influence of environment must be very little. Children are truly helpless; they are surrounded by adults who are so much more strong and clever—adults who have generations of experience in how to manipulate children and condition their responses. The child as an individual hardly stands a chance.

This observation is not to be interpreted as a judgment; it is simply a description of what appears to take place. We generally call it "education." More accurately it is "civilizing the human being."

Whatever, the child does in fact develop and present to the

outer world a collection of qualities which the world calls his "personality." However most children realize quite clearly (and often quite early) that this so-called personality is not the essential "I", but rather an impersonation (or, more accurately, a collection or series of impersonations somewhat similar to the costumes of a quick-change artist) which the "I" must present to "That-other" if his wants and needs are to be fulfilled.

We call that end of the psyche which relates to the outer world the *persona*. Persona means "mask" and is indeed an apt title for this function. In ancient Greek drama actors spoke through masks which depicted the character and the emotion they were portraying. The mask was obviously not the real person of the actor; it represented a part he was playing for the sake of the drama. The audience did not see the actor himself on the stage, it saw only his persona. As the emotions and character of his role changed, the actor would change masks correspondingly.

Likewise it is my persona which stands between "I" (my ego) and the outer world as a sort of actor's mask. It is through my persona that I relate to the outer world. If I want to relate well and successfully to the outer world ("That-other"), if I want to "make it" in my culture and society and have my wants fulfilled and my needs met, I will present to the outer world the persona which I perceive the outer world wants to see and will accept. That, of course, will change as "That-other" changes —perhaps even several times a day. Moving from one situation to another, from interaction with one person to interaction with another, I may change personas (masks) several times in a short period of time. Thus the comparison to the quick-change artist, rapidly slipping from one disguise to another, is quite appropriate.

The development of the persona is a very real necessity. If

children were left to develop according to their natural tendencies without benefit of education and guidance, they would mature into little more than monsters. In our society we tolerate behaviors in toddlers which otherwise we consider inappropriate. It may not be desirable but it is at least tolerable for Joey the tot to kick the next-door neighbor in the shin because he is justifiably angry with him. But that must change with time. If Joey the teenager or young adult kicks the next-door neighbor in the shin because he is justifiably angry with him, Joey is liable to be in for serious trouble. It may not be desirable but it is at least tolerable for Janet the tot to snatch candy from a playmate and eat it. But that must change in time. If Janet the teenager or young adult snatches food from another person's cafeteria tray and eats it, Janet is liable to be in for serious trouble.

Somewhere in between Joey the tot and Joey the teenager, Joey must become educated, cultured, and civilized. He must learn that expressing anger by kicking the neighbor in the shin is taboo in our society. He must learn another way to express his anger— a way that is appropriate; a way that will conform to our society's customs and values. This new way will be a persona for Joey. As Joey the young adult, he may still *want* to kick the neighbor in the shin to express his anger, but will rather relate to the neighbor through his mask (persona) and verbally confront the neighbor in an appropriate manner, a manner acceptable to society. Essentially the same is true of Janet.

Unfortunately another possibility exists for Joey and Janet. In the process of their personality development they may not be given the opportunity to shape a healthy and appropriate persona. They may not learn that there *is* a behavior acceptable to "That-other" which will achieve the same end as the tot behavior which is no longer acceptable. They may instead learn that the tot behavior is unacceptable in *any* shape or form and must be denied and repressed completely. Joey may learn that being angry is wrong, that he is a bad boy when he is angry, and that he must not get angry. Joey will thus develop a persona that will mask his natural anger *completely*. When he feels anger (which of course he cannot admit), he will smile rather than frown and he will justify rather than confront whatever it is that has raised his anger. Janet may learn that wanting things is wrong, that she is a bad girl to want things, and that she should be content with what she has. Janet will thus develop a persona that will mask a healthy ambition and valid desire for gain with a front of smiling satisfaction and contentment or even subservience.

Because the source of input and influence in the process of civilizing children is so extensive and inclusive (parents, family, school, church, etc.), the possibility of undesirable results is real indeed. It is quite likely that given the unfortunate experiences I have just described for Joey and Janet, they will probably become neurotic personalities to some degree and be less than happy in their experiences of life.

The development of persona is obviously not a simple task. In the process of our personality development we are very much like a winding stream: we want to follow the path of least resistance and, frankly, go the way that is easiest for us. Still, early on we realize that way may not be acceptable to society ("That-other") or at least will not facilitate meeting our needs. Therefore there is an inevitable bind: on the one hand we want to be ourselves, do our thing, be natural (kick the nasty neighbor in the shin); yet on the other we want to "make it," be accepted, look good, or, as we say, "put our best foot forward." The result is that in the process of personality development there is an inevitable compromise taking place in every one of us—a degree of falsification. We compromise what we are with what our society expects us to be. And this compromise is our persona.

I said earlier that it appears the human psyche by nature contains *in potential* all possible human traits or characteristics of personality. Also there appears to be a law of psychic balance whereby when one quality is drawn into the end of the psyche which relates to the outer world (persona), its opposite quality is dropped back to the other end of the psyche which is closer to the inner world. It stands to reason, then, that if desirable qualities fairly well fill the persona end of the psyche so that the best foot is put forward for the outer world's acceptance, the other end of the psyche which relates to the inner world is going to contain an assorted collection of qualities opposite those desirable ones up there in the persona.

It would seem that this end of the psyche, closer to the inner world, is rather dark and foreboding. And indeed it is. It is called the *shadow* because it is by nature the opposite of the brightness of the persona. Whereas the persona stands between the ego and the outer world and relates the ego to the outer world, the shadow stands between the ego and the inner world and relates the ego to the inner world.

To get a partial image of shadow, imagine a person who is essentially a kind, peacemaking individual to his friends and acquaintances. He is identified by them as a loving and forgiving person who is generous, wants to help people, and could even be said to be selfless. His purity of morals is evident and he is a quiet, submissive type of man. That would be a description of this man's persona.

By definition, the shadow is the opposite of the persona. Therefore this man's shadow would contain a sour, disruptive quality. It would be hateful and vengeance-seeking. It would be greedy, selfish, and would probably want to hurt people. It would be lustful and controlling.

Not only are qualities opposite the persona present in the shadow, they are present to a comparable degree. The more strongly a quality becomes lodged in the persona, the more strongly its opposite is constellated in the shadow.

The shadow is like a foreign personality—a primitive, instinctive, animalistic kind of being. It is the collection of uncivilized desires and feelings that simply have no place in cultured society. The shadow is everything we don't want to be. Or rather it is perhaps everything we would *like* to be but don't dare. The shadow is everything we don't want others to know about us. It is everything we don't even want to know about ourselves and have thus conveniently "forgotten" through denial and repression.

Denial and repression play a big part in the development of personality and the civilizing of the child. They are generated by the "shoulds" and "oughts" and "musts" of the growing-up process. Joey learns that he "should not" kick the neighbor when he is angry with him and Janet learns that she "must not" snatch and eat her friend's candy. You don't do those things because they are not "nice." This becomes reasonable and generally acceptable to Joey and Janet in time because they realize that without such admonitions kids would grow up to be "bulls in china shops"—impulsive actors-out of raw feelings. If everyone in our society behaved that way there would be absolute anarchy.

Consequently, one by one, these impulses, reactions, and feelings which are rather primitive and certainly unrefined but very natural to the human being get relegated to the shadow (kicked down the cellar stairs and a heavy door slammed shut on them), and appropriate behaviors and words which are acceptable to society are nudged onto center stage.

One of the most common mistakes people make is to believe they have successfully gotten rid of all that primitive savagery. In fact, all that has happened is that it has been successfully repressed into the unconscious where it resides as vitally as ever. We all keep stored away in our shadows the multitude of qualities and dynamics which did not pass muster to get into the persona.

The magnitude and intensity of the shadow will vary from person to person but will be largely related to the growing-up experience of the person. There is an inverse relationship between the size of the shadow and the atmosphere or milieu in which the person was reared: the more expansive the milieu, the smaller the shadow; the more restrictive the milieu, the greater the shadow.

People who grow up in an expansive atmosphere—one that is accepting, open, compassionate, nonlegalistic, relaxed, confident, and structured with reasonable limits—have fewer things to repress and consequently do not develop massive shadows. They learn the fundamentals of their family's and of their society's customs and values, but they are relatively free to be and become themselves within the parameters of responsible propriety. They learn appropriate expression of feelings and consequently do not have to repress them. Because they learn to be comparatively self-confident and develop a positive and healthy self-image, they are not as dependent upon society's approval and may thus be less inhibited, but still within the bounds of propriety. Much of what would otherwise be shadow stuff in their psyches is integrated into their personalities.

On the other hand, people who grow up in a restrictive atmosphere—one that is narrow, demanding, closed, legalistic, tense, rigid, and suppressive—have a great many things to deny and repress because of the multitude of "musts" and "dare nots" integral to their growing up. There are so many thoughts they are not allowed to have, so many words they are not allowed to speak, so many behaviors they are not allowed to perform; and these must all be repressed. The value of society's approval is of significant importance in this type of milieu. There is little room for curiosity or experimentation; consequently these dynamics must be repressed into the shadow. Spiritual experience in such a milieu is often legalistic piety which likewise demands repression of much of that which is natural to the human experience. All in all, persons developing in such an atmosphere generally end up with massive and intense shadows and thick personae.

Most of this foregoing material has to do with what is called the *personal* shadow and some with what is called *collective* shadow. By definition the personal shadow includes drives, experiences, images, and fantasies that were repressed for personal reasons during the course of the individual's development. Aggression and sexual perversion are common elements of the personal shadow. Doubt and rebellion may be commonly present in the shadows of religious persons.

The collective shadow is similar except that it is comprised of that which is repressed because it is taboo to the society in which the person belongs. What your culture disallows becomes the common content of your collective shadow. In the current era of liberation movements the suppression of persons would be a part of our collective shadow. Hatred and rage are also common elements of the collective shadow.

Beyond the personal and collective shadow is yet a third dimension, the *archetypal* shadow. It is the archetypal shadow which provides energy to the personal shadow and the collective shadow. It is the presence of evil which resides deeply and innately in every human being; hence the classification of archetype. Without question, human beings are capable of great good; but the opposite always resides within our archetypal shadow—*we are likewise, each of us, capable of horrendous evil.*

Nevertheless, it is unjust to view the shadow only as dark and evil. There are many qualities that are undeveloped or underdeveloped residing in the shadow. Often in the second half of life they begin to come forward into consciousness because the person is not as firmly focused on the outer world as he was in the first half of life and consequently has time to look inward. Remember, too, the opposites of what appear in the persona also reside in the shadow. A person who develops negative attributes in his persona may have a lode of gold hidden in his shadow.

We shall see repeatedly in the pages that follow that the befriending of one's shadow creates great positive potential for the person who is willing to do it. Continued avoidance and denial of one's shadow makes a person dangerously vulnerable to it.

Walter Hilton, who was the Augustinian canon of Thurgarton in the 14th century, produced an account of his spiritual journey which he titled *The Scale of Perfection.* In a fascinating way Hilton described the movement into the darkness and evil potential of the shadow. But he included a somewhat unexpected although not really surprising observation. He wrote:

> But what shalt thou find? Surely this: a dark and painful image of thy own soul, which hath neither light of knowing nor feeling of love nor liking. This image, if thou behold it wittingly, is all bewrapped with black stinking clothes of sin as pride, envy, ire, accidie [sloth], covetise, glutony and lech-

ery. This image and this black shadow thou bearest about with thee wherever thou goest. Out of this image spring stirrings of pride, of envy and such other, the which cast thee down from the honesty of man into a beast's likeness. Peradventure now thou beginnest to think with thyself what this image is like and I will tell thee. It is like no bodily thing. Verily it is nought, or no real thing. This nothing is nought else but darkness of conscience; a lacking of love and light, as sin is nought but a wanting of God.

Nevertheless in this dark conscience it behoveth thee to labour and sweat; and then when thou findest right nought but sorrow and pain and blindness in this darkness, if thou wilt find Jhesu thou must suffer the pain of this dark conscience and abide awhile therein. For within this nought is Jhesu hid in his joy, whom thou shalt not find with all thy seeking unless thou pass this darkness.

From the Christian point of view Hilton's observation is quite orthodox. Understanding and accepting that within myself I have the potential for the greatest evil, the blackest of sin, increasingly magnifies my awareness of God's grace. And, as Hilton says, if you avoid this encounter with your dark and evil shadow, you will never really find Jesus in his joy.

2

SHADOW
and myth

To achieve personal wholeness or completeness and to become a well-integrated person is a noble goal toward which most human beings strive. However, because of the way we have been taught, most of us are persuaded that this goal is achieved through the continued infusion of goodness and righteousness, the development of a finer morality, and the successful abandonment of evil.

There is certainly truth to this observation, but I believe it is only a partial truth.

The thesis of this book contends that one moves toward the achievement of wholeness, completeness, integration, or perfection in the sense of the Greek word *teleios, not only* through the continued infusion of goodness and righteousness, *but also* through the acceptance, "owning," and conscious incorporation of one's shadow into one's self. I am indeed *not* a complete person until I incorporate into my conscious self that dark side of my person which is every bit as much a part of me as that bright self, that persona, which I parade before the world.

According to orthodox dogma (as well as the morning newspaper), the human being is a creature capable of great good *as well as* great evil. Not everyone, however, is ready to affirm this. History is filled with stories—legends, myths, tales, accounts—of how a person moves forward towards wholeness and completeness only when he succeeds in ceasing to avoid or deny his shadow or evil side of himself and instead acknowledges it, becomes acquainted with it, and makes friends with it. Nevertheless, it seems that Christianity has been rather resistant towards accepting this concept. I believe Christian people know the wisdom of this intuitively, but hesitate to deal with it consciously because it may appear to be "courting the devil." To make friends with your shadow or to embrace your shadow (as I like to imagine it) would be, they say, merely a prelude to going to bed with it (or identifying completely with it). The thought of taking something of dark or negative quality and incorporating it constructively into your Christian life is, to say the least, threatening.

In actual experience it is the opposite which is true: the person who repeatedly denies and represses the shadow is much more vulnerable to its power and much more likely to be overcome by it than is the person who makes friends with his shadow and uses his darkness constructively.

There are countless illustrations of this in literature; one is particularly fascinating. It is a medieval German legend of the 15th century and concerns a dark but enlightening version of the life of one of the fathers of the church, Saint John Chrysostom.

Saint John Chrysostom was born in Antioch around 345, and became patriarch of Constantinople. He gained the title John Golden Mouth because of his sermons in which he reached a height of oratory unparalleled in early Christianity. However, because of his ascetic zeal and his attacks upon the luxury of his day, he was sharply criticized by his peers, banished twice, and finally died in exile in Asia Minor at the age of 62. The version of the legend which I am about to retell appears in Heinrich Zimmer's collection of tales of the soul's conquest of evil *The King and the Corpse.*

The story is told that a great many years ago there was a pope of Rome who made a habit of riding horseback through the woods accompanied by his knights. On regular occasion he would leave the group, go off by himself, and bow his head to recite his prayers. On one of these occasions he heard a voice crying pitiably somewhere in the woods. He interrupted his prayers and rode off in the direction of the sound, seeking the person but finding no one.

Unable to find any being there in the woods, the pope suspected that the voice must be that of a ghost. Sitting still in his saddle he called out, "In the name of God, declare yourself." The voice answered mournfully, "I am a miserable soul suffering in the flames of hell."

Wishing somehow to help, the pope asked how he might relieve the poor thing of its pain. "Oh, I am afraid you cannot," said the voice. "But there is in the city of Rome a woman, the wife of a pious and just man, who is pregnant with a child whose name will be called John when he is born. This child will become a priest; and if that priest will say 16 masses on my behalf, I shall be freed from this damnation." The tormented soul told the pope where he could find these parents-to-be and, in an instant, was gone.

Returning to Rome, the pope immediately located the man and his wife and inquired as to when she would deliver her child. They agreed with him that he should care for the child, so when the boy was born the pope took him into his protection, christened him John, and cared for him as his own son.

When John began school at the age of seven it was apparent that he was quite unable to do well in his studies and was indeed the brunt of mockery by his fellows. John was shamed by this and so began to offer special prayers to the image of Our Lady every morning when he went to church, asking her to help him in his work. One day in the midst of his prayers he observed the lips of the image move and he heard the Virgin say, "John, kiss my mouth and you shall be filled with knowledge to become the master of all arts." John was frightened by this experience, but the image encouraged him not to be afraid but to do what he was told. He drew forward, pressed his trembling lips to the mouth of the Blessed Virgin, and by that kiss took unto himself wisdom and a marvelous knowledge of the arts.

When John returned to school from his miraculous experience, he settled down to listen and learn, but soon realized that he did indeed know more than all the others in the school put together. There appeared a golden circlet around his mouth which shone brightly. His schoolfellows were dumbfounded when they saw and heard, and demanded to know what had taken place that he was suddenly so brilliant. John related his experience to them and on hearing of the miracle they gave him the name Golden Mouth. Thereafter it was John Golden Mouth who did all the teaching at the school.

As the years went on the pope grew increasingly impatient to release from hell the suffering soul he had encountered that day in the woods, and he sought to have John ordained as soon as possible. At the age of 16 John celebrated his first mass, but in the midst of it was strangely disquieted within himself. It occurred to him that he was extremely young to be a priest and to commune thus with God. Truly he was not at all prepared and he began to fear that he would certainly regret this day forever. So he vowed there in the midst of the mass that he would be poor for the sake of God and that whenever the mass was ended he would run to the wilderness and there remain a hermit as long as he should live.

As soon as the banquet following the mass had ended and everyone had rejoiced over the early ordination of John Golden

Mouth, the young man quietly slipped away, clad in poor clothes and carrying nothing more than a loaf of bread. When the pope learned of John's disappearance he was greatly upset and went immediately with his knights to search everywhere for the vanished prodigy. But in vain, for John had built himself a well-camouflaged hut deep in the wilderness beside a spring and at the edge of a cliff, and could not be found. Subsisting on roots and herbs, praying, fasting, and continuous in devotion, he remained at his hermitage and served God day and night.

Not far from the forest in which John had reclused, there lived an emperor comfortable in his castle together with his family. One day the emperor's daughter, along with the young ladies of her court, went out to gather flowers. Suddenly a gale arose with winds so strong that it lifted all the frightened maidens high into the air. When the winds subsided and they were set down again, they discovered that the princess was not among them, nor could they determine in which direction she might have been blown. Quite sad, they told the emperor of what had happened and he immediately began to search diligently and extensively, but to no avail. The beautiful royal maiden could not be found.

What had actually happened was that she had been set down by the gale winds precisely at the threshold of John's hermitage, lost and bewildered but quite unhurt. She looked inside, and seeing John kneeling at his prayers felt confident to call to him. He was alarmed to see her and upset that she should be there, but he was persuaded within himself to admit her, believing that he should be guilty before God if he permitted her to die of hunger or to fall prey to the animals of the forest.

Nevertheless, he took his staff and drew a line across the floor of the hut, dividing it in two. One side he assigned to her and commanded her not to cross over it, but to stay on her side and to live such a life as would befit a proper recluse. She agreed, and for a time the two continued side by side in this way, praying, fasting, and serving God. The tempter, however, envied them their life of sanctity and succeeded one night in encouraging John to cross the line and take the girl in his arms, whereupon the two slipped to the ground, their bodies meshed in embrace.

After that, they were smitten with remorse. John feared that if the girl should remain with him it would happen again; so he quietly led her to the edge of the cliff and gently pushed her over. But the moment he had done this he suddenly realized that he had sinned even worse than before, and he cried out, "Oh, miserable, accursed wretch that I am; I have murdered this innocent girl! Had I not seduced her she would never have thought of sin; and now I have taken from her her life. Oh, God will indeed avenge my sin forever!"

In great despair and hopelessness John left his hermitage and began to move out of the wilderness. As he did he began to feel a strain of hope within himself and decided to confess his sins. He made his way to the pope, gained his audience, confessed his sins, and professed repentance. But the pope, his godfather, did not recognize John and turned him away in a terrible outburst of indignation. "Get out of my sight," he said. "You have dealt as a *beast* with that innocent girl; your sin be on your head!"

Deeply afflicted by what he perceived as the pronouncement of God, John returned to his hut where he fell to his knees and made a solemn vow. "May God," he said, "whose mercy is greater than my sin, accept with grace the penance I now impose upon myself. I vow to walk on all four limbs, as a beast, until I have merited God's grace; and God in his mercy will let me know somehow when I have atoned for my sin."

And this he did. He went down on his hands and moved about on all four limbs. Nor would he draw his body up to a standing position, but when he was tired would creep into the hut and lie down as a beast. He existed in this manner for many years, and his garment rotted and fell away, and his skin grew rough and hairy, and to the eye he was no longer recognizable as a human being.

In the meantime it so happened that the wife of the emperor (whose daughter had been swept up by the gale) gave birth to another child and the pope was asked to baptize it. All appropriate preparations were made, but when the pope took the infant in his arms it cried out loudly, "No! You are not the one to baptize me." The pope was astonished and frightened and tried to quiet the infant, but the babe persisted in its resistance. Finally it said, "Saint John the holy man is the one who shall baptize me. God will send him to me from out of the wilderness." At that the pope, still bewildered, returned the child to its nurse and went to the empress asking who the Saint John was who was to baptize the infant. But neither she nor anyone else knew.

About this very time, the emperor's huntsmen with their hounds ran down a very curious beast which was beyond their recognition. However, since it gave no resistance they easily captured it, throwing a cloak around it and binding its legs. They brought it to the castle of the emperor, and as the rumor of it swept among the people many came to look at it. The creature, however, shied away from the curious onlookers and sought to hide under a bench.

Among those seeking to get a look at the strange sight was the nurse with the emperor's child. Quite suddenly the infant commanded: "Let me see the beast." One of the servants prodded it from its hiding place, and twice it made its way back into hiding, but the third time remained out in view.

Then the infant addressed it with a firm and clear voice: "John, Saint John, I am to be baptized by your hand."

The beastlike creature softly but firmly replied, "If you speak the truth and your words are the will of God, say again what you have said."

34

"Dear Father," said the infant, "why do you wait? I tell you I am to be baptized by your hand."

At this John called aloud to God asking that God should let him know by the voice of the child if his sins were atoned. And the child continued: "Rejoice, dear John. God has forgiven all your sins. Rise up now, and in the name of God baptize me."

As John obeyed, and stood up from his beastly position, the filth and scale that clung to his skin began to fall away like withered bark and his body became clean and smooth again. The servants brought him clothing and the pope and nobles gave him welcome.

When John had baptized the infant he said to the pope, "Do you not recognize me, dear father?" The pope replied that he did not. John continued: "I am your very own godchild; you baptized me with your own hands, sent me to school, and while I was yet very young you ordained me a priest. But as I was celebrating my first mass I became aware of how inappropriate it was for me to take the host into my unready hands. So after the mass and following the banquet I quietly slipped away into the wilderness where lo these years I have prayed and suffered and sinned and repented." John went on to describe and confess how he had seduced the young woman and murdered her.

The pope told the emperor the story, and as he heard it his heart grew very heavy with sadness. He asked John to lead him to the cliff where the girl had been killed, that they might recover her bones and provide them a decent, Christian burial. John agreed and led a party of huntsmen through the wilderness to the edge of the cliff. As they peered over the brink they saw a young woman quietly sitting below.

John called down to her: "Why are you sitting there alone at the foot of this cliff?"

She called back, "Do you not know who I am?"

John replied, "No, I do not."

"I am the one who came into your hut," she said, "the one whom you threw over the cliff. No harm came to me because God bore me up."

John was amazed; for it was as by a great miracle that she sat there, beautiful as she had ever been, and clothed in royal garments. She returned to her home accompanied by the party, and her father and mother took her to their hearts and gave thanks to God for her recovery. The pope and John departed to return to Rome.

On the way, the pope asked, "How many masses have you said, my son?"

"Just that one," John replied.

"Oh," said the pope, "I am filled with anguish that that poor soul is still suffering in the fires of hell."

But John knew nothing of the pope's experience years ago in the woods and asked to what he referred.

Then his godfather described to him the encounter of that day and John learned he could redeem that suffering soul by saying 16 masses. "That is the reason why I brought you up to be a priest," said the pope.

John, without hesitation, offered up one mass a day for 16 days and the suffering soul was indeed released from its pain. And, the legend declares, the pope eventually made John a bishop, for he filled his office with humility and devotion, and his sermons were like necklaces of gold so that he was once again called John Golden Mouth. He wrote many books about God, and when his ink ran out, says the legend, he would go on writing from his mouth, and the letters that flowed were indeed the purest gold.

Before we proceed to look into the wisdom of this tale, it is necessary to realize that in myths, legends, and fairy tales there is usually much more present than meets the eye. And, as is often true in real life, things are not always what they seem to be. We have here the marvelous account of how one person experienced the awareness that "only the sinner can become the saint." And we see that those aspects of our human nature which we are prone to describe as evil, devilish, or at least dark and undesirable may in fact be the very stuff which brings us closer to completeness by thrusting us into the light of divine grace.

Interestingly enough there is a strong taste of the theology of Martin Luther in this legend. Even though the tale was first in print nearly a score of years before Luther was born, it carries the flavor of what was to become somewhat thematic to Luther—a strong awareness of the reality and influence of sin and evil and an even stronger awareness of the grace and mercy of God given directly to a man or woman through the merits of Jesus Christ. For Luther, being in touch with one's dark side was extremely important and beneficial for life. In 1515 he wrote these comments on Romans 6: "If sin attacks but does not dominate it is forced to *serve the saints.* Thus wantonness makes the soul more chaste by its attack; pride, more humble; laziness, more active; avarice, more liberal; anger, more gentle."

The problem in the legend is that John had become too good too quickly. A fantastic collaboration of the powers of heaven and hell with the authorities of earth had brought him well along the path of saintly perfection while he was yet an adolescent, and a protected adolescent at that. His godfather, the pope, had hurried him into priesthood at the earliest possible moment, apparently without giving much thought to the earthly wisdom of such a move. John, however, seemed to possess a sort of intuitive wisdom which told him that, despite the marvelous and miraculous experiences of his brief life, it was not quite right that he should stand at the altar of God, communing with God and dispensing the grace of God in the form of the sacrament of the Holy Eucharist. "I am much too young," he said to himself. "I am yet too innocent; I have not experienced life."

Young John is indeed to be commended for feeling moved by his own conscious sense of inadequacy and insufficiency to the point of deciding that he must cease his priestly functioning. As a priest he should be one who "knows" life, and he does not. To absolve sin he should be one who knows what sin is, and he does not. Though the pope himself approves him and lays his hands on him, still John feels ineligible.

He is intellectually aware of the great importance of integrating into his character the wisdom of an experience of the dark powers and evil forces from which he has been protected both by his rearing under the wing of the pope and by the innocence of his unassuming nature. Innocence, as we shall observe later, may indeed be a desirable characteristic, but it may also be a very dangerous one. Still, John cannot anticipate what misery and pain he will encounter on that dusty and jagged pathway of integration through experience. And indeed, if he could, would he do it? So such ignorance is desirable—yes, even necessary.

John becomes his own physician, his own counselor, and prescribes for himself the treatment for his condition; he goes off into the wilderness of life to learn to "know" it. But not without the companions of honesty and sincerity and humility and unselfishness. They accompany him and allow him to continue to hear his own intuitive voice as he gropes along the way to his completeness.

Now he is closer to the primitive. In the wilderness he is closer to the beast residing beneath his outer garb of innocence. If he is to effect his cure he will need to bring this neglected primitive into consciousness through living experience—and it happens. Some of the basic, elemental forces of existence, of which he was quite unaware in his innocence, break through from his shadowy being and John is overwhelmed. In his remorse for his sexual act he fears that he will indeed sin again and again unless he somehow puts away the object—the young princess. But he resolves his problem in the basest manner possible, literally throwing her out of his sphere of experience. The resolution, however, only serves to make matters worse, for more than ever he experiences the full impact of the foul and evil counterpart to his sweet and innocent self, and discovers the depth of devilishness actually existent within him.

He becomes a beast. He physically enacts the very semblance of the beast residing beneath his outer appearance. He literally becomes what he has *found himself to be;* what was before his mark of identification now rots and falls from his body and he keeps only to his filthy, mangy, brutish existence.

Then comes the summons from the higher forces. God himself, who had never abandoned John through his descent into the subregions of experience, calls to him through a yet unbaptized infant, and releases him from his self-prescribed atonement, assuring him of his rebirth, his completeness, his sainthood.

The legend depicts how important and necessary it is for us humans, for the sake of growth toward wholeness and integration, to endeavor to welcome into our conscious selves that dark and murky shadow side comprised of everything that superficially we are *not.* John Golden Mouth had never invited into his conscious experience these negative qualities, these elemental forces, these aspects usually designated as undesirable and indeed to be shunned by anyone who is "good." Not only had he never in his innocence sought to embrace them, he was protected from them and very quickly cast into the highly dignified role of priest. By virtue of the extreme superhuman and human favor shown him, he found himself in a position for which he intuitively felt totally inadequate. And this is his salvation—that he did not blindly accept this role which was thrust upon him and go about in proud arrogance (however subtly manifested) and superficial piety, but that he questioned its propriety in the light of his experience. "Who am I to handle the mysteries of God and distribute to men the assurance of his grace which conquers all sin? Such merit within me is completely unattained. And even though I be endowed with all wisdom and knowledge and be able to transmit this profoundness through golden oratory, yet do I know that I know nothing. Until I walk through the valley of the shadow myself I will never 'know' the human situation—I will be only a part of a person."

John was right. Though he had been declared a redeemer even before he was born, he had to *become* before he could fulfill his mission.

3

SHADOW
and Jesus

Jesus of Nazareth was one of the greatest supporters of the concept of making friends with the shadow side of your personality. Throughout the gospel accounts of his dealings with people, he appears consistently as one who knew firsthand the workings of the human being. His wise and insightful teachings include an understanding of wholeness that does not exclude those negative elements and qualities that to many of his day (and ours as well) seemed undesirable, if not in fact disgusting. Especially significant, I believe, is the advice he gives to his followers (the 12 disciples) as he prepares them to go two by two on their first mission of teaching and healing (Matthew 10).

In some detail Jesus instructs his men to go specifically to the "lost sheep of the house of Israel" to carry out their mission of teaching and healing. But he warns them that theirs is a dangerous mission because he knows from his own recent experiences that a great many people in the house of Israel are not at all receptive to what he has to say, but are in fact hostile toward him and his message. He has found that this is particularly true of the highly influential religious leaders. He warns his men of the danger of their mission, telling them that they may meet not only rejection, but even persecution. Never being one to beat around the bush, he levels with them straightforwardly, and in striking imagery right in the midst of his instructions he says to them: "Behold, I send you out as sheep in the midst of wolves" (Matt. 10:16).

How would you like to hear words like those concerning your first major assignment from your boss? Everyone knows that sheep are no match for wolves. Wolves are known to do sheep in. And Jesus is no dummy—he knows that too. What he does is to point up very clearly the reality of their situation, so that they are not fooled but know what they are getting into. But he does not leave it there; he goes on.

How shall the sheep go; in what manner? Shall they go into the game blindly, naively trusting the people to whom they are commissioned to bring the good news of the new covenant? Definitely not!

Shall the sheep at least go into the game knowing what the rules are? Hopefully!

Shall the sheep go to beat the wolves at their own game? Well, now—maybe that is a little *too* much.

Jesus continues: "Look out for people! Don't let yourselves be overcome by their sophisticated craftiness! Keep up your guard! Be foxy!" Only Jesus chooses other animals than the fox —he chooses the serpent and the dove. "I send you out as sheep in the midst of wolves," he says, "so be wise as serpents and innocent as doves."

Be wise as serpents and innocent as doves.

There is something fascinating about this imagery; the disciples are to carry themselves into this situation, this encounter with the world, with the wisdom of a serpent and the innocence of a dove—qualities which *seem to be* precise opposites of each other. Perhaps they are. And perhaps this is one of the basic reasons for Jesus' advice—take both and be complete.

In ancient myth and lore the serpent was an emblem of cunning and wisdom. The serpent appears, for example, in Genesis 3:1, and is described by the writer as follows: "Now the serpent was more subtle [clever] than any other wild creature that the Lord God had made." It was this serpent who, according to that account, deceived Eve with its cleverness; the result of which was Eve's and ultimately Adam's gaining of the knowledge of good and evil—a raising of their consciousness and awareness.

Through the centuries the serpent became identified with the devil. The Apostle Paul (2 Cor. 11:3) makes this identification, and it becomes particularly clear in the Apocalypse, The Revelation to Saint John (12:9 and 20:2): "And the great dragon was thrown down, that ancient serpent who is called the Devil and Satan, the deceiver of the whole world—he was thrown down to the earth, and his angels were thrown down with him" (Rev. 12:9).

Furthermore, crafty hypocrites are also called serpents in the New Testament as, for instance, when Jesus in the midst of lashing out against the scribes and Pharisees says, "You serpents, you brood of vipers, how are you to escape being sentenced to hell?" (Matt. 23:33).

In all these references in the New Testament, the Greek word for serpent is *ophis*. This parallels the Hebrew word for serpent which is *nachash*. In fact, in the Septuagint (Greek) version of the Old Testament, the word *ophis* is used in the Genesis 3:1 verse. The connection between "serpent" and "devil" seems clear enough.

In Jesus' injunction to his disciples the Greek word *phronimos* is translated "wise" ("wise as serpents"), but it also means "intelligent, prudent and mindful of one's own interests." The word *akeraios,* generally translated "innocent," also means "without admixture of evil" and "free from guile."

Just one more note: the word describing the serpent in Genesis 3:1 is *arum,* and may be translated "crafty, subtle, shrewd, clever, ingenious."

My reason for this excursion into words is this: It would appear that Jesus' advice to his followers is a marvelous piece of wisdom, albeit somewhat alien to the 20th century Christian consciousness. In essence you hear him knowingly say to his disciples, "As you go out now to live and witness in the real world of people, who may very well be hostile to you and your message either overtly or covertly, endeavor to be as wise, crafty, shrewd, subtle, clever, and ingenious as the devil himself; and yet, be as innocent, simple, pure, and free from guile as a dove. Incorporate the dark, shadowy counterpart of shrewdness and cleverness (definite attributes of the devil) into the light of sweet innocence."

"Make friends with your shadow!"

These men need to be in touch with the *whole* of the experience of life, and Jesus knows that. They will be incomplete and thus inadequate if they go off solely in blind faith and trust. Not unlike Saint John Chrysostom they will only be complete and whole men if and when they bring into conscious awareness those aspects of their own selves which to "godly" people would seem dark and highly undesirable and indeed to be suppressed, and *use* those aspects constructively in carrying out their mission. Innocence must be mingled with craft. They must take with them a godly innocence—a purity, a fidelity, a trust, a righteousness—*and* they need to take with them a caution, a crafty wisdom or shrewdness, a critical, even skeptical, eye. They need to know the ways of God *and* the ways people work against God.

They need to know the power of darkness *as well as* the power of light.

Nor is this account of Jesus' wise advice to his followers a remote facet in his teaching. A study of Luke 15:1—16:13 quickly reveals the marvelous wisdom and insight which Jesus possessed about human nature. It, like the foregoing account, clearly illustrates a facet of Jesus' concept of the nature of good and evil which may have escaped much of Christianity.

Luke records the setting to be a fairly typical one for Jesus. The people of the world, that is, the tax collectors and sinners (the "scum of the earth"), had gathered around Jesus to listen to his fascinating teaching. These people were so termed— "scum of the earth"—by their traditionally religious counter-parts, the Pharisees and scribes—persons whom Jesus despised largely because of their blatant hypocrisy and their persistent denial, suppression, and repression of their *own* evil.

Jesus proceeded to tell them the famous "lost" parables: the lost sheep, and the lost coin, and the lost son (or prodigal son as he is so frequently called). The thrust of these stories concerns the great rejoicing which takes place among people when they *find* something they had *lost.* The parallel he draws is that when a person goes his own way and, through willful violation of his loving relationship with God and his fellow men, sins, he becomes like the sheep and the coin and the son: lost from the fold, from the collectivity (of the coins), from the family (the household). But when, somehow, the lost one is returned to a loving relationship with God and his fellow men, he is back in the collectivity and there is rejoicing and celebration by God and his angels and all of heaven.

Then Jesus went on to tell them yet another parable, and it is this which concerns us. In this parable we see him again as a worldly-wise human being. In the previous parables he applauded the virtue of righteousness and the avoidance of sin and evil, and gave the explicit impression that this is desirable and to be cultivated by his followers. He now goes on to tell them that, on the other hand, *un*righteousness may not be without its virtue as well, and it will be to the distinct advantage of his followers to incorporate the dark counterpart of cleverness and shrewd planning into the light of purity and innocence.

The story concerns a certain wealthy entrepreneur who had employed a steward or manager of his enterprises. Now I would suspect that being a rich man, this fellow was probably very shrewd (the wealthy entrepreneurs in Jesus' stories are invariably clever and tough and never have the wool pulled over their eyes), and being a shrewd man it is no surprise to find that one day he discovered that his manager was guilty of mismanagement of his assets. Precisely what the crime of mismanagement was or how the manager had committed it is of little import. What *is* important is that the entrepreneur acted immediately; he was not one to tolerate any skulduggery. He called the manager into his office and said to him point-blank, "I have become aware that your management of my accounts has not been to my best interests. Therefore, you will produce a complete account of the handling of my property, for you are no longer fit to be a manager in my employ."

Obviously the man was guilty of the charge because he left his boss' office without a word. But it was only as he left that the full impact of it all began to settle upon him. "I'm fired," he said to himself. "I am thrust into the ranks of the unemployed. What do I do now? I'm not strong enough for a job of manual labor, and I'm certainly not going to lower myself to begging."

But as he pondered his problem a solution began to shape up in his mind. "I know what I'll do," he said. "I still have some

46

time before I turn over my books to the boss. I'll get myself in good with as many people as I can. I'll get them in my debt so I can guarantee some real security for my future." So he settled on the old political ploy of "I scratched your back, now you scratch mine"—a favor for a favor.

But what favors did this now-jobless rogue have to bestow? Ah, a great many indeed! He called together a number of farmers and businessmen who were in debt to his employer and he took them aside, one by one. To the first he said, "How much do you owe my boss?"

The man replied, "A hundred barrels of oil."

"Tell you what," replied the manager. "Because I like you I'm going to let you sit down there right now and write out a check to him for 50 barrels of oil, and that will settle your account in full."

When the next debtor came, the manager said to him, "How much do *you* owe the boss?"

"A thousand bushels of wheat," was the reply.

"Well, for *you*," said the manager, "write out a check for 800 right now, and I'll mark your debt 'Paid in full.' "

And on and on it went.

Being the type of man he was, I would suspect that the entrepreneur was angered when he first heard of the manager's trick. But his anger soon turned to more of a well-I'll-be-damned attitude. Before long his feelings for the manager actually shifted to the range of admiration, because when he finally called him in to confront him with his deed he actually commended the man for his cleverness, his prudence, and his ability to look out for himself (albeit at *his* expense).

With the story ended, Luke goes on to record Jesus as adding a brief commentary on his parable. It is in his commentary that my chief interest resides. Jesus is reported as saying, "The master commended the dishonest steward for his shrewdness, for the sons of this world are more shrewd in dealing with their own generation than the sons of light. And I tell you, make friends for yourselves by means of unrighteous mammon, so that when it fails they may receive you into the eternal habitations" (Luke 16:8-9).

There are indeed a great many interpretations of Jesus' commentary on his story, and most of them focus on the right use of wealth and prudent planning for one's spiritual future. I am tempted to say that is not really the thrust of Jesus' parable here, except that what he is recorded as saying following the above quotation seems to nail down this interpretation quite adequately. In Luke 16:10-13 Jesus adds,

> He who is faithful in a very little is faithful also in much; and he who is dishonest in a very little is dishonest also in much. If then you have not been faithful in the unrighteous mammon, who will entrust to you the true riches? And if you have not been faithful in that which is another's, who will give you that which is your own? No servant can serve two masters; for either he will hate the one and love the other, or he will be devoted to the one and despise the other. You cannot serve God and mammon. [Most modern translators render the Greek word *mamona* as "money" rather than "mammon."]

Perhaps Jesus is endeavoring to get across several messages in his story about the dishonest steward. I believe he is. But I also believe that the message which may bear the greatest significance for human beings receives the least attention by commentators and interpreters in general: namely that message which has to do with the desirability of embracing one's dark or shadow side and the unification of opposites in one's personality. It is reasonable, however, that this should be the case, for it tends to underscore the general reluctance on the part of traditional Christianity to encounter in a positive way the dark side of our humanity and learn from it.

In this parable Jesus clearly demonstrates his wise understanding of human beings and he endeavors to get this across to his followers. He tells the story of a shrewd and crafty person—a crook in fact—who is precisely the *opposite* of what is traditionally held to be goodness and righteousness. The man, by his silence in the face of his accuser, appears indeed to be guilty of the crime of embezzlement or mismanagement or kickback or whatever, even though no specific evidence is mentioned in the story. Therefore he appears as a "bad guy" or a "child of darkness," or a "man of the world," as opposed to being a "good guy" or a "child of light" or "otherworldly."

However, the hearer begins immediately to perceive this manager as a man of mature reflection, for already in his soliloquy he manifests his ingenuity. His resultant action is further evidence of his astuteness as he goes about feathering his nest, insuring his future security at the expense of his boss. When he is apprised of the manager's actions, the boss not only ignores the manager's further dishonesty but actually commends him for his shrewd foresight.

Jesus then injects a sort of assessment, which may appear to be an aside but which, I believe, strikes at the heart of the matter. He makes a comparison between the "sons [children] of this world" and the "sons [children] of light." In traditional Christianity the children of this world represent the ungodly, the unrighteous, the materially minded. The Greek word *aion*, which in this case is translated "world," has an ancient meaning of "to breathe or blow" and denotes "that which causes life—a vital force." Next, the word means "age," "a lifetime," "life itself." And finally, considering the word to be the aggregate of things contained in time, *aion* is translated "world" or "universe."

Now the New Testament tends to identify a distinct difference between "this *age*" and "the *age* to come" or between "this *world*" and "the other *world*" or "the *world* to come." The dividing line is the return of Christ. The "age" or "world" prior to Christ's return is characterized as being a period (place) of instability, weakness, impiety, wickedness, calamity, and misery. Children of this world, then, are those who are controlled by the thoughts and pursuits of this present time, and the New Testament writers, in general, censure them. Later Luther, in his *Small Catechism,* lumps together "the devil, the *world,* and our sinful self" as an unholy trio which might prevent the coming of God's kingdom and deceive people, leading them into sin (Lord's Prayer, Third and Sixth Petitions).

Nevertheless, regardless of the multitude of negative connotations, there is still that ancient meaning of *aion* which must be reckoned with: "that which causes life—a vital force." At the root of that which appears to be totally negative lies something very positive.

The children of the world in Jesus' parable are compared to the children of light. The Greek word for light, *phos* or *photos,* is often used poetically in metaphor and in parable. Thayer's lexicon comments that "the extremely delicate, subtle, pure, brilliant quality of light has led to the use of *phos* as an appellation of God. It is also used of that heavenly state, consummate and free from every imperfection, to which the true disciples of Christ will be exalted. It is used to denote truth and its knowledge, together with the spiritual purity congruous with it.

And finally, *phos* is used of one in whom wisdom and spiritual purity shine forth."

From this brief journey into etymology it should be fairly clear that Jesus' commendation of anything about the children of the world is somewhat radical. That is unless he recognizes the "vital force" concept of *aion,* and realizes that any person who is *all* light (or believes that being all light is most desirable) is an incomplete person. In fact, he seems to *chide* the children of light for their unsophistication in handling the affairs of life. It is clear Jesus' intention is that his followers should learn and incorporate into themselves something important and necessary from the children of the world—something which, for the most part, is entirely too lacking in them. For example, this manager, who is indeed a genuine child-of-the-world type with all its dark connotations, does not for one moment conceal from himself the greatness and immediacy of the danger which threatens him. Contrast that with the self-deceiving tendency often observable in children of light who deny and repress reality; who make themselves vulnerable to all sorts of forces because in their naivete they remain ignorant of the gravity of the situation.

Second, note that the manager thinks immediately and carefully about ways and means to insure his future. When means come to mind which seem unsuitable, he rejects those in order to consider better ones. He is quite clear within himself as to what he desires, namely, to continue living in a relatively easy and secure way. He employs much of what we would in modern terms call "the method of effective problem-solving." Contrast this with the carelessness, lack of planning, and blind trust which may be observed in children of light who tend toward sluggishness, irresolution, and lack of sophistication because they believe that the pursuit of spirituality is higher and better than any other pursuit.

Third, the manager is obviously inventive (shrewd, clever, astute, prudent, wise, seeks his own interests). But he doesn't stop with mere projects and plans. He acts! He carries out the plan which seems to him to promise the richest rewards and completes effectively the method of problem-solving. Contrast this resoluteness with the loitering and procrastination sometimes observable in children of light who lag in acting in the matters of life because they believe that "things will work out" or who have no time because they are too busy practicing virtue purely for virtue's sake.

Jesus holds up the manager as an example for the children of light. I do *not* hear him say, "You, now, go out and steal and cheat and covet material wealth." But I *do* hear him say, "You, my disciples, my followers—children of light—you need to study your dark counterpart. You need to look at some of the attributes manifested in this manager, this symbol of your dark counterpart. You need to incorporate and integrate into yourself some of those attributes which he manifests. You *have* those attributes in your shadow, but you neglect to develop them because you are afraid they will smudge your goodness and dim your light. No, just the opposite; they will help you become more whole and complete human beings.

"Frankly, there is a crook in every honest man. Now that does not mean that every honest person must *become* a crook. But my story tells you that you may use in an honest way elements that may be characteristic of a dishonest person. So I say to you, season your innocence and naivete with shrewdness and sophistication. Infuse the 'shady' into your light; all goodness and light alone will leave you only incomplete.

"And when you have so embraced your shadow you will know

and be entrusted with some of the true riches of greater completeness and wholeness, higher consciousness and awareness. You must *embrace* your shadow, but you cannot lie with it. To do that is to become its slave. And you cannot serve two masters."

It seems to me that the parable of the Dishonest Steward greatly reinforces the observation that Jesus recognized clearly: there is indeed something substantially positive and desirable to be gained by embracing that which is commonly thought to be negative. In other parables, too, he speaks positively of qualities and attributes which are generally considered to be negative and undesirable. For instance, the story which is commonly called the parable of the Importunate Friend recorded in Luke 11 holds up the attribute of dogged persistence and tenacity. Likewise the parable of the Unjust Judge in Luke 18 also speaks to the positive value of being a pest. The two stories differ only in their setting; they seek to make the same point.

In the first story, it is midnight as a man knocks on the door of his neighbor, seeking to borrow bread to feed an unexpected guest who has just arrived. Because the neighbor is in bed and has finally got his noisy family settled down for the night, he is extremely reluctant to get up for *any* purpose. Nevertheless, granting the favor turns out to be less trouble than continuing the argument. So he ends up giving the man some of his bread because the man simply will not stop pounding on his door.

The second story concerns a certain judge who reportedly had no respect for God and little regard for man. A widow of the city kept coming to him asking for justice in the case against her adversary. Even though the judge cared nothing about the woman or about justice, he nevertheless finally vindicated her simply to get rid of her continual nagging.

I suspect that parables such as these sometimes shock people who are "sentimentally religious" or "spiritually otherworldly." The point or lesson of these parables is indeed a pious one, namely that people are encouraged to be persistent in their pleas to God. Jesus stated that himself. Yet I cannot help but believe that there is more to these stories than just that. At least *my* experience of life leads me to believe that there is. In fact, I wonder if he told them with a straight face or with a smile, because it seems to me that there is definitely a humorous and satirical twist to them.

It may be considered by some of the children of light that it is a desirable virtue to be quietly accepting; and a vice to be self-assertive. Indeed it is an integral part of Jesus' ethic to be non-resistive. (Matt. 5:39ff.) Yet is there anything in these two parables that speaks to incorporating assertiveness from the shadow into the conscious behavior of everyday life? I believe there is. And how far removed is this from his exhortation to adopt the attitude of the unjust manager in terms of wisdom and prudence?

I believe we see many times in the teaching of Jesus of Nazareth such encouragements to make friends with our shadows. However, in much of the later history of Christianity, such an emphasis on moral perfection as the ultimate goal developed that there was (and is) a strong tendency to lose sight of the fact that true wholeness and completeness—the *teleios* (perfection) of which Jesus spoke (Matt. 5:48)—necessarily includes acknowledging and coming to grips with the shadow side of goodness, and finding a way even to embrace it.

4

SHADOW
and innocence

There appears to be an innate fear of the dark in most of us. Perhaps it is because in the dark we cannot see and consequently cannot protect ourselves from hurting ourselves or being hurt by others. Perhaps it is because of the disorientation we feel when we cannot get visual bearings on where we are, and we are uncertain as to where our foot will come to rest on our next step. Or perhaps we are afraid of the dark simply because from very early in life we *learned* that we *should* be afraid of it; it was always associated with that which was scary, spooky, potentially harmful. Criminals committed crimes "under cover of darkness." People did "bad" things in the dark so that they wouldn't be seen—things they would be ashamed to do in the light. Darkness was always synonymous with anonymity. Darkness was equated with ignorance.

Darkness has consistently received rather bad press. Consequently it isn't too surprising that darkness, as well as that which is associated with it or symbolized by it, should not be found to be too attractive to people—especially "good" people. "Not good" people might be more attracted to it because according to what we learned, they are the types who would prefer it to cover their deeds.

Perhaps this is the reason so many people avoid coming to grips with their shadow and instead continually deny and repress it. Perhaps their experiences with darkness have been bad, and all they have learned about darkness has been scary; so consequently they are not about to risk anything that might get them anywhere near that which is not well illuminated. I know several people who refuse to express anger and instead deny and repress it. The reason, they say, is that the only model they ever had for expressing anger was a destructive one. In other words, their image of expressing anger is hitting, beating, screaming, and smashing things. According to them, they never witnessed constructive, healthy confrontation and conflict. The only way they know to express anger is destructive, and since they don't want to be destructive, they simply don't become angry. (Actually they do become angry, but deny and repress it so that it never gets acted upon.) Similarly, something of the same dynamic may take place with people who avoid and deny their shadows.

In addition to achieving the basic goal of steering clear of that which is frightening, this avoidance and denial appears to many to be desirable and commendable. It is true that people who never express any anger are rewarded for being calm, even-tempered, tolerant, and long-suffering. Likewise people who deny their shadows are identified as sweet, innocent, righteous, and sometimes even godly. Feedback such as this is obviously a positive payoff and is quite desirable even though the person may not consciously be seeking it. Behavior which gets such reinforcing is probably going to be repeated, and thus a pattern is established which gets progressively more difficult to break.

As with most things it may begin very early in life. In the

training program of growing up, children are told "be good" and "don't be bad." This is, of course, commendable instruction; one would hardly encourage parents to instruct their children to "be bad." Most children do not have to be instructed to be bad; they will be bad by their nature.

But not all. As we shall see, some will so totally repress their badness (for a variety of reasons) that they will appear as absolute angels, pure and innocent as the driven snow, perfect children, with no vices or evils *at all*. On occasion these children have been known to murder people (often parents and siblings) quite at whim, and are said to have had something "snap" within them. They sometimes have no recall of their actions and appear to be in a daze, and others wonder what came over them. Sometimes they kill themselves. Friends who knew the young person report that "he was a model child," "well-mannered and behaved," "really a perfect young man," and "the *last* person we would have expected to do anything like *that*."

Encouraging children to be good and not bad *is* indeed commendable. But we need to remember the law of opposites in personality development: the more we strive for something bright, the more its dark counterpart is constellated unconsciously. The more that innocence and goodness get reinforced into the persona, the more their opposites build up in the shadow. *This does not mean abandoning striving for something bright; it simply means remaining conscious of the corresponding happening in the psyche.*

The quality of innocence remains a virtue. Yet there is innocence and again there is innocence. Herman Melville, that master storyteller who wrote *Moby Dick,* also produced a classic short story of innocence and murder titled *Billy Budd, Foretopman.* The time of the story is the end of the 18th century, during the

French and English Napoleonic wars, just after the Great Nore Mutiny.

It is the summer of 1797 when Billy Budd, age 21, who is aboard a homeward-bound English merchant ship, is impressed from it into service aboard the outward-bound H.M.S. *Indomitable* which had of necessity put to sea short of her proper complement of crewmen. In what becomes the dominating characteristic of his personality, Billy complies with the impressment with "uncomplaining acquiescence."

Indeed Melville works diligently to portray Billy as the epitome of sweetness, purity, and innocence. He "looked even younger than he really was, owing to a lingering adolescent expression in the yet smooth face, all but feminine in purity of natural complexion, but where, thanks to his seagoing, the lily was quite suppressed and the rose had some ado visibly to flush through the tan."

Even in his name one may see the child carrying over into adulthood—the diminutive "Billy" rather than Bill or William. And is it too much hypothesizing to suggest in the name "Budd" a possible parallel—that he is still a sweet and tender bud, not an opened, grown blossom? Whatever, Melville calls him "virginal" and "angelic" and has one of the old sailors aboard ship refer to him as "Baby Budd."

As would be expected, Billy is conscientious and cheerful as well as being strong, and soon becomes the center of virtually every group aboard ship. He seems to have the virtue to sweeten even the sour sailors. Everyone loves him; that is, everyone except John Claggart, the 35-year-old master-at-arms, the "chief of police" who is responsible for preserving order on the lower gun-decks.

Melville describes Claggart as being possessed by the "mania of an evil nature, not engendered by vicious training or corrupting books or licentious living . . . but born with him and innate; in short, 'depravity according to nature.' " He is perhaps the only man aboard ship who is "intellectually capable of adequately appreciating the moral phenomenon presented in Billy Budd." In one sense Claggart is attracted by Billy, but in a much larger sense he is grossly repelled by the very sweetness and innocence which is mildly inviting.

One night while Billy is asleep on deck, a shipmate approaches him and begins to ask for help in planning a mutiny. Billy becomes righteously indignant and puts aside the proposition. However, as is generally true of such good and sweet persons, he hates to hurt another's feelings and consequently is reluctant to, indeed almost incapable of, giving a clear message of "I want no part of it" to the shipmate. Furthermore, he says nothing of this to anyone.

Shortly after this incident Claggart accuses Billy of planning a mutiny, and the captain of the ship, Edward Fairfax Vere, calls him in. Not knowing the purpose of Captain Vere's summons, Billy in his innocence fantasizes only positive reasons why the captain might be calling him—perhaps, for instance, an appointment to a better post aboard the ship. When, however, he hears Claggart recite his accusation before the captain, he is so overwhelmed that he can only stammer, and cannot get one intelligible word out. At first the captain demands that he speak up and defend himself; then perceiving Billy's impediment of stuttering under stress, he says, "There is no hurry, my boy. Take your time." Instead of putting him at ease, this genuine concern only makes Billy block all the more. Rage wells up inside him and all his passion surges into his right arm. He lunges out at Claggart, hits him a terrific blow squarely in the forehead, and kills him almost instantly.

Though he recognizes his innocence, Captain Vere realizes

that Billy must hang for his "crime," and it must be done quickly, else the entire British fleet might become involved in new mutinies that would disrupt the whole order of state. So Captain Vere makes his decision and a drumhead court convicts Billy and sentences him to death. At dawn the next morning, from the main yard of the ship, Billy is hanged.

Now, was Billy overtaken by some outside force or power? Was he momentarily possessed? Or insane? In any other court could he have pleaded temporary insanity? Or is there in Billy perhaps a tragic flaw which leaves him very vulnerable?

He is too good to be true! He is in fact *not* true, and he is overcome by his own evil, his own shadow. In his lifetime he had consistently, unconsciously denied and repressed his shadow in order to retain his sweet innocence. Then he used his sweet innocence to protect him from self-awareness and any insight into his own darkness. The cycle would thus be completed and then repeat itself.

Melville notes that generally a child's "innocence wanes as intelligence waxes." But such was not the case with Billy Budd. "Experience is a teacher indeed," said Melville, "yet did Billy's years make his experience small. Besides, he had none of that intuitive knowledge of the bad." His great deficiency is that he is incapable even of comprehending, let alone coping with, evil.

Innocence in children is a very normal and natural characteristic. We say children are sweet; we are moved to protect them because of their lack of experience and sophistication. "Don't take candy from strangers," we tell them. "Don't get into the car of some stranger who offers to give you a ride." We hope, however, that they will grow and mature into being able to be aware of these things and protect themselves.

When this childlike innocence remains, for whatever reason, and we see it in an adult, we are often sensitive to ambivalent feelings in ourselves, being on the one hand somehow intuitively attracted to this sweetness and purity (as was Claggart to Billy); yet also feeling a vague uneasiness, that somehow *because* this person appears too good to be true, we are being "put on" or even "used." Often there is a feeling of uneasiness being in the presence of such a person, and we want to move physically away from him.

In a very real sense, Billy Budd appears as a combination of Adam and Christ. Melville records Captain Vere as seeing Billy as a "fine specimen of the genus Homo who in the nude might have posed for a statue of young Adam before the Fall." Also, Melville designs that Billy shall fit the pattern of the vicarious sufferer—Christ in his crucifixion. In fact, just before Billy is hanged, he shouts, "God bless Captain Vere."

The important thing in this descriptive figure of the Adam/ Christ is that it further points up Billy's ignorance of evil. Unlike Christ's innocence, Billy's innocence is made up (as was Adam's before he ate the fruit) of his lack of knowledge of good and evil—his lack of conscious awareness of evil. It was not, like Christ's, the result of a profound insight into the world and humanity.

Throughout the story Melville so emphasizes Billy's ignorance and naivete as the main ingredients of his innocence that he appears almost animallike, nearly deprived of a moral faculty. One might conclude that he was almost hopelessly unable (unfit?) to exist in the world of humanity—that he would never "make it." For example, he is dedicated to becoming so shipshape that he will please everyone and *never* merit criticism or reproof; he frets over his failures inordinately; he persists in gullibly believing in the charitable disposition of Claggart, even though the old Dansker sailor warns him thoroughly to the contrary; he demonstrates a total lack of perception of the ramifications of the vaguely mutinous plan suggested to him by his shipmate; and he shows his severe lack of discretion in failing to report the incident to his officer.

Given all this it is not surprising that when at last he stands before his captain, falsely accused by Claggart of inciting mutiny, Billy Budd can neither comprehend nor cope with the evil; he is struck dumb and cannot speak. Since he cannot speak, he acts, and the only act he knows (barbarianlike, animallike, out of his archetypal shadow) is a blow. The Christlike Billy, which obviously was not the *authentic* Billy, disappears, and he answers with a solidly human—no, even demonic—fist. Like Ahab, another of Melville's striking characters, Billy's only response to evil is to lash out and annihilate it. But again, like Ahab, Billy becomes inextricably enmeshed in the very evil he would destroy. *His own evil, with which he is not at all in touch, overcomes him in his seeking to destroy evil; and in so doing, it destroys him.* The monstrous shadow has broken through the heavy oak door, bounded up the steps, and devoured the cream-faced innocent. Darkness has overcome light.

It would be quite possible and not at all difficult to discount this account of Billy Budd as merely a tale. Which is, of course, *always* possible—except to do that is simply to join the ranks of Billy Budd. The innocent are hard to convince even though the Billy Budd story has been lived out thousands of times over in actual life and reappears with regularity in our newspapers and on our television newscasts. If people do not *want* to believe in the potential evil power of their shadows, they won't. What they *will* do though, in their naivete, is make themselves vulnerable to being overcome by them. It has been said many times that the devil is not offended when he hears a person deny his existence; in fact, he is delighted. It is much easier to move in on someone when that person believes you don't even exist.

In an intuitive fashion if in no other way, we occasionally or regularly get the notion that there is indeed a power (shadow) resident within us which can take hold of our ego and use us as a pawn or tool. And just precisely when we lie back assuring and complimenting ourselves that we have successfully withstood being overcome by it, we are overcome by it. The insidiousness of it all is demonstrated in one of *The Screwtape Letters* of C. S. Lewis (Macmillan, 1967). Lewis has Screwtape, a senior devil, correspond with Wormwood, a junior devil, concerning the latter's efforts to win a "patient" away from Christianity. At one point in the process Screwtape writes,

My dear Wormwood: The most alarming thing in your last account of the patient is that he is making none of those confident resolutions which marked his original conversion. No more lavish promises of perpetual virtue, I gather; not even the expectation of an endowment of "grace" for life, but only a hope for the daily and hourly pittance to meet the daily and hourly temptation! This is very bad.

I see only one thing to do at the moment. Your patient has become humble; have you drawn his attention to the fact? All virtues are less formidable to us once the man is aware that he has them, but this is specially true of humility. Catch him at the moment when he is really poor in spirit and smuggle into his mind the gratifying reflection, "By jove! I'm being humble," and almost immediately pride—pride at his own humility—will appear.

Increasing purity and innocence does not immunize one from evil. The more the shadow is denied the stronger it becomes. Consider Sam. Sam was just a little boy when his father died. His mother told him that now he must be especially good because there were just the two of them and she would not be able to handle things if he gave her any trouble. So Sam became good—very good, in fact. Too good to be true, you might say. But things went well, and the living was easy.

More quickly than he expected, Sam's mother remarried, but the new marriage was not a good one for the little family. Still, Sam remained the good boy, *never* causing any trouble, excellent student, regular church attender, properly groomed, properly mannered, quiet, well-liked, athletic, always in control. Sam exercised control, not to impress others, but because he believed it was right to do so. Unlike other young teenagers, he never tested limits. Whatever he did, he did the way he believed it ought to be.

On one particular evening, 15-year-old Sam quietly got ready for bed, dressed in his pajamas, and turned on the television set in his room. He sat down on his bed, watched the program for a moment, then got up and took down from the wall a souvenir machete which had been given to him by an older cousin. He called his mother to come to his room and as she entered the door he struck her with the machete; in horror movie genre, he literally "chopped her to pieces." He was later found wandering the streets, quite oblivious to what had happened.

The people who knew Sam "couldn't believe" what had happened. "No one would *ever* have expected Sam to do that; other kids maybe, but not Sam." "I just can't imagine Sammy doing anything like this." The next-door neighbor said, "I'd trust that kid until hell freezes over."

When these tragedies occur, and they occur quite regularly, the stories are usually similar. The person is described as an absolute saint—again, too good to be true. Friends and neighbors are overwhelmed by the "impossibility" of the news and very often say what the one person said of Sam: "No one would ever have expected *Sam* to do that; *other* kids maybe, but not

Sam." The irony in this is that the Sams in our society are precisely the very people who have the greatest potential for being overcome by their powerful, destructive shadows and for consequently acting out murderous/suicidal behaviors. The "other kids" who are continually testing limits and giving parents, teachers, preachers, et al., one fit after another—these anything-but-too-good-to-be-true kids—also possess the potential for murderous/suicidal behaviors, but are much less likely to be overcome by their shadows because they are in much closer communication with them than are the Sams. The Sams, for all practical purposes, believe they have obliterated their shadows and are only their personas; that is, they believe they *are* only what they appear to be. When this happens to a person, or rather when a person brings this about, he is then most vulnerable to being overcome.

For 24 years Alice had been a faithful and obedient housewife to a tyrant of a husband. The word *obedient* is unfortunately appropriate in describing Alice because she earnestly believed that was her true role—to obey her husband and fulfill his wants and needs.

Shortly after their marriage Alice realized that the man with whom she had fallen in love had successfully misrepresented himself to her, and she with her vision impaired by "lovesickness" had seen in him only what he wanted her to see, and certainly what she herself wanted to see. But she had been mistaken, and 24 years had verified the "discovery" she made about her mistake.

Frank was a mean man. His growing-up experience had been suppressive, and Frank dealt with his experience by becoming resentful and self-centered. He believed that some day he would get even with life. In Alice he found a willing servant—a slave to carry out his wishes and satisfy his needs. So it wasn't long after he had succeeded in "acquiring" her that he laid aside the facade of tenderness and caring and said to her, "OK, now we can be our real selves."

For 24 years Frank was true to his goal to "get even with life" and he carried out his striving for it chiefly through Alice. He was extremely self-centered, his wife and children were *always* secondary to his own desires, he was consistently short with Alice, he would embarrass her publicly, shout at her, and on many occasions he physically abused her.

Throughout the marriage Alice remained the loyal wife and obedient servant. She *never* gave public indication of dissatisfaction, unhappiness, or anger. She was a consistently pleasant woman whose constant reply to the questions, "How are you, Alice? How are things going with you and Frank?" was a smiling, "Fine; we're doing just fine, thank you." She publicly supported Frank in many of his behaviors and excused him in view of his "hard childhood."

It happened on New Year's Day. The family was gathered at Alice and Frank's and were all assembled in the family room watching parades and football. Alice, by herself, was in the kitchen preparing the meal. She had just taken a huge ham out of the oven where it had been baking and was about to slice it when Frank appeared at the doorway. She knew he had drunk several cans of beer during the TV viewing and wasn't surprised that he bumped into the door frame coming into the kitchen. He came to her, grabbed her by the upper arms, and threw her against the counter as he yelled, "When in the hell are we gonna eat, anyway?"

Her reaction was instantaneous. She drew back her right arm and before she or Frank knew it she had plunged the carving knife deep into his chest with the full force of her being. Frank gasped and fell to the floor, his eyes still wide open in amazement, the knife handle protruding grotesquely from his bloody shirtfront. Alice backed away slowly, stared down at the lifeless body, and whispered, "My God in heaven, what have I done?"

Twenty-four years of shadow broke through in one instant. Twenty-four years of denied and repressed disappointment, resentment, anger, and rage overcame Alice's guardians and controls, smashed through that figurative oak door which locked in her dark side, and culminated in murder. Twenty-four years of "innocence" was obliterated with one stroke.

Alice never dealt with her personal shadow—she ignored and denied it. So it handed her over to a greater enemy, the archetypal shadow. And every time the archetypal shadow succeeds in swallowing the ego, an individual's values are disintegrated, he is overwhelmed and overcome by the unconscious, and he is bereft of energy to resist it.

I said earlier in this chapter that there is innocence and again there is innocence. The word means "not harmful." That is the true virtue of innocence. The innocent remain unstained by guilt, but that does not mean that the innocent do not know what stain *is,* or how guilt may come about. True innocents are able to carry childlike attitudes into maturity while still being realistic in their perception of evil.

On the other hand there is the manufactured innocence produced by the wearing of rose-colored glasses and blinders, naivete, lack of sophistication, unawareness, immaturity, refusal to come to grips with and to terms with the "demon" of evil and destruction in one's self or in others. This kind of innocence has no sense of suspicion or distrust—no doubts, just unfailing (blind) faith. It sees only the good, and in true Pollyanna fashion believes and hopes only the best. It is always the optimist, always the positivist.

But this "innocence" turns out to be nothing more than a

mechanism of defense, a strategy by which to make it through life. Some people are impressed by it (especially other innocents), others ignore it, some are turned off by it as inauthentic, and a few actually attack it. Regardless, all it does for the person is make him extremely vulnerable to forces within and without himself which he believes do not even exist.

Many people were shocked when Stanley Milgram's book *Obedience to Authority* (Harper & Row, 1974) was published. Milgram, a social psychologist and researcher, had demonstrated experimentally that when a human being can pass the responsibility for his evil over to "responsible" authority figures who command him to do violence, most will do it. Milgram says,

> . . . ordinary people, simply doing their jobs, and without any particular hostility on their part, can become agents in a terrible destructive process. Moreover, even when the destructive effects of their work become patently clear, and they are asked to carry out actions incompatible with fundamental standards of morality, relatively few people have the resources needed to resist authority.

Milgram's research was criticized by professionals and nonprofessionals alike, largely because of what the critics termed "unethical experimentation" and "hoodwinking of subjects." My suspicion is, however, that a substantial amount of the criticism was defensive behavior—a strong wish for reality to be other than it actually is, a wish to deny the tremendous potential for evil actually residing within common, ordinary, moral people.

Hans Askenasy, who himself spent years in Germany under Nazi persecution, picked up Milgram's thesis and, in the light of it, examined the Nazis who carried out the murder of six million Jews. Askenasy concluded that they were neither madmen, sadists, nor monsters. In fact, at the Nuremburg trials Adolph Eichmann was certified to be normal by a half dozen psychiatrists, and his lawyer stated he had the personality of a "common mailman."

Many people are still convinced, however, that those Nazis *were* madmen or monsters. If that is true, then the responsibility for the horrible atrocities they committed can be placed on a special class of maniacs or criminals. But Askenasy titled his study *Are We All Nazis?* (Lyle Stuart, 1978), indicating his own rejection of that myth and intimating his bitterness toward society's moral passiveness and even denial in the face of such evil potential.

Being afraid of the darkness in one's self and recognizing the dangerous power potential in it is no sin or crime, and certainly nothing to be ashamed of. In fact, it is quite reasonable. It should be obvious that coming to grips with the evil side is no picnic in the afternoon sunshine. It may very well be a powerful and frightening experience. But true spirituality rests a great deal on experience. It brings a person more in touch with himself; it expands and deepens his consciousness. True spirituality says to the innocent, "Do you realize what you are up against? Do you realize what it is all about? Or are you some kind of naive rube?" Certainly this was part and parcel of Jesus' instructions to his disciples to be innocent as doves, but also to be wise as serpents.

It is interesting to note here that normal children seem to be in quite a hurry to "grow up"—to leave the stage of innocence, to get over or get past it into more mature sophistication. It is as though there is an innate awareness that innocence is a rather vulnerable state to be in; that built into normal innocence is a tendency for it to lose itself.

Experience demonstrates that the reality of life *is* that as one's capacity for joy, happiness, and peace increases, so does his capacity for woe, pain, and strife. Undifferentiated or unidentified growth can never alone be the basis for a way of life or even a goal towards which to strive. Growth may be evil as well as good. Students coming into a program of clinical pastoral education often naively identify a personal goal of the training experience to be growth—"I want to grow." The assumption is that they want to become more aware of and gain new insights into themselves personally, and that they want to increase their skills as clinical ministers. The assumption is also that they will accomplish this in a purely positive and desirable experience without any pains, agonies, or frightening discoveries.

This is, of course, a desirable expectation, but quite unrealistic. Human existence is both joy and woe, happiness and pain, peace and strife, success and failure, loyalty and treason, and all the possible opposites. What a person *intends* will not always be good but sometimes evil. The demon in me (which is *my* demon) will struggle and clamor to be heard often, and indeed will be heard sometimes. But the more I am acquainted with him, aware of his presence, and respectful of his power, the less likely I am to be overcome by him.

"Love your enemies" is indeed an admirable command, but it demands a tremendous amount of grace. Not that it is impossible, for indeed it is not. But I do believe that Jesus of Nazareth who gave this command to his followers was well aware of the difficulty of fulfilling it even as he gave it.

Some Christian people, hearing this command and perhaps unconsciously registering its difficulty, tend to become very moralistic. Love then becomes a kind of moral exercise, a routine of character-building calisthenics which further blocks awareness of how really difficult it is and how much it requires grace. Inauthenticity and artificiality, if not indeed hypocrisy, are the results of this moral effort, which sometimes is an *extreme* effort because some enemies are *extremely* difficult to love. And the result is very different from what Jesus originally intended.

A Christian man was talking with me once about the effort expended in loving the unlovely. He said, "I simply approach the person saying to myself that I *do* love him, when deep inside I think I know that I do not love the man at all, but am in fact disgusted by him. And yet I feel good that I can follow our Lord's command." How conveniently we block our demons from our awareness and end up devoid of authentic spirituality but saturated with slushy sentiment and syrupy self-righteousness!

Being afraid of the shadow, the darkness, and the power potential in it is no sin or crime and nothing to be ashamed of. But closing your eyes in the darkness neither increases your safety nor improves your vision. Repressing and denying your shadow through manufactured innocence will only make you more vulnerable to its power.

Make friends with your shadow; for we achieve good not apart from evil, but through it; even in spite of it.

5

SHADOW
and St. Paul

I do not understand my own actions. For I do not do what I want, but I do the very thing I hate. Now if I do what I do not want, I agree that the law is good. So then it is no longer I that do it, but sin which dwells within me. For I know that nothing good dwells within me, that is, in my flesh. I can will what is right, but I cannot do it. For I do not do the good I want, but the evil I do not want is what I do. Now if I do what I do not want, it is no longer I that do it, but sin which dwells within me (Rom. 7:15-20).

Paul, apostle to the Gentiles, author of a substantial and influential portion of the canon of the New Testament, and zealous enthusiast for the gospel of Jesus Christ, has succeeded in encapsulating in these few sentences one of the greatest of human confessions, as well as perhaps one of the most significant of human projections. I suspect that no one will quarrel with the bulk of that observation, but I likewise suspect that not all will agree with the last dozen words.

In this well-known passage, as well as in other less-familiar passages, Paul recognizes and admits to another power within himself which brings about actions and behavior contrary to his good conscious intentions. Certainly this is commendable because it brings to his conscious awareness the presence of his shadow within him. But why does he choose to refuse to accept it as a part of himself? Why does he instead project it onto "sin" and declare that it is not after all *himself* at the root of this discomfort, but *sin?* It sounds very much like Paul wants to deny this shadow from being a legitimate and inevitable part of his total being. If this observation is accurate, then the only recourse is somehow to cut the shadow off from one's self. But as we have seen, relegating the shadow stuff to the unconscious resolves nothing; it only makes the person more vulnerable to its increasing power.

A very convenient way of "getting rid" of something undesirable is to throw it away. This is precisely what we do with our shadow when we refuse to come to grips with it: we throw it (project it) onto other people, things, or events. We find it humorous to hear the comedian quip, "The devil made me do it," after he is confronted for a wrongdoing. We laugh at his rationalization and avoidance of personal responsibility. Intellectually we can see his projection. But which is easier to say? "The devil made me do it," or "It is no longer I that do it, but sin which dwells within me"?

Saul of Tarsus was a fanatical enthusiast for Pharisaic law; indeed he soundly identified it with the ancestral Jewish faith. Because of what he perceived to be the heresy of fledgling Christianity, he became a bitter and hostile persecutor of the Christian church, bent on utterly destroying it. On his way to Damascus for the purpose of wiping out the Christian congregation in that city, Saul of Tarsus was miraculously converted to Paul, apostle to the Gentiles. His experience appears to be a classic turnaround of 180 degrees—a full and complete reversal and movement in the opposite direction. In describing the man on the basis of his recorded epistles, the venerable commentator John Peter Lange said Paul was a man "burning in his love for the Lord and his brethren; and for this very reason overpowering in his moral indignation and rebuke of all that was opposed to the honor of his Master."

It would seem that after his conversion Paul was as zealous *for* Christianity as he had previously been *against* it. Likewise, as Lange suggests, the strong feelings he held towards Christianity before his conversion may possibly have been directed towards Christianity's *opponents* after his conversion. A suggestion of this occurs in the fifth chapter of his letter to the Galatians:

> For freedom Christ has set us free; stand fast therefore, and do not submit again to a yoke of slavery.
>
> Now I, Paul, say to you that if you receive circumcision, Christ will be of no advantage to you. I testify again to every man who receives circumcision that he is bound to keep the whole law. You are severed from Christ, you who would be justified by the law; you have fallen away from grace. For through the Spirit, by faith, we wait for the hope of righteousness. For in Christ Jesus neither circumcision nor uncircumcision is of any avail, but faith working through love. You were running well; who hindered you from obeying the truth? This persuasion is not from him who calls you. A little leaven leavens the whole lump. I have confidence in the Lord that you will take no other view than mine; and he who is troubling you will bear his judgment, whoever he is. But if I, brethren, still preach circumcision, why am I still persecuted? In that case the stumbling block of the cross has been removed. I wish those who unsettle you would mutilate themselves! (Gal. 5:1-12).

Obviously Paul is angry. He is very upset by the Judaizers who followed him and are trying to persuade the new Galatian converts to Christianity to take up Jewish practices, including circumcision. "You were doing fine," he says. "Who is it that is messing you up? This business of having to be circumcised is not *my* teaching. If I were teaching *that,* why would I still be persecuted? No. You tell those who are disturbing you that I would like to see the knife slip!"

Now we really do have to admit that is a rather nasty fantasy or wish—that Paul's opponents who are so bound on declaring circumcision to be a "must" would accidentally *castrate themselves.* But who among us cannot identify with such a feeling? To have someone walk behind us deliberately knocking over every article we have set up is infuriating. So the feelings and the response are indeed understandable.

What is *not* so understandable, however, is Paul's inability or seeming refusal to be aware of the sharp contrast between this vengeful wish and his repeated admonitions to Christians everywhere *always to show and practice only love and patience.* Paul is extremely zealous in his letters to the young churches in urging them to think and behave only out of their "light" side. He drives this home repeatedly, and there is a degree of reasonableness to it. Parents tell children to "be good," not to "be bad," and the children learn to "be good" through precept and especially example. In the same way Paul, parent to his Christian children, instructs them to "be good" (he knew he would never have to tell them to "be bad"—they could accomplish that quite easily on their own, particularly in a pagan world where few standards of morality existed). Following the above passage from the Galatians letter he instructs:

But I say, walk by the Spirit, and do not gratify the desires of the flesh. For the desires of the flesh are against the Spirit, and the desires of the Spirit are against the flesh. . . . Now the works of the flesh are plain: fornication, impurity, licentiousness, idolatry, sorcery, enmity, strife, jealousy, anger, selfishness, dissension, party spirit, envy, drunkenness, carousing, and the like. I warn you, as I warned you before, that those who do such things shall not inherit the kingdom of God. But the fruit of the Spirit is love, joy, peace, patience, kindness, goodness, faithfulness, gentleness, self-control; against such there is no law. And those who belong to Christ Jesus have crucified the flesh with its passions and desires. . . . Let us not grow weary in well-doing. . . . As we have opportunity, let us do good to all men.

Whatever became of the *struggle* he so clearly identified in Romans 7:15-20? It would appear in these injunctions that the *struggle* between "doing good" and "the desires of the flesh" is nonexistent. His ethic seems to be totally one-sided— the development of a collective persona and the repression of every human trait which contradicts this persona. In Romans 12 he says: "Repay no one evil for evil, . . . never avenge yourselves, but leave it to the wrath of God" (vv. 17-19). In Philippians 2 he says: "Do nothing from selfishness or conceit, but in humility count others better than yourselves. Let each of you look not only to his own mistakes, but also to the interests of others" (vv. 4-5).

These are all certainly high ideals to which Paul admonishes us. And he is definitely right in asserting that to act out our impulses—the desires of the flesh—in complete license is destructive, even demonic. But the issue is not nearly so much a matter of allowing lawless and irresponsible actions as it is finding a way to deal with the tendency towards the direction of darkness (the real presence of the shadow). Repressing the shadow side from consciousness only encourages a one-sided identification with the light side (the persona). Paul's zeal is so strong that hearers are encouraged to become and *believe* they have become (are) their personae. This, as I have repeatedly tried to demonstrate, is a terribly tenuous position to be in.

The matter of struggle and tension evident in Paul's personal identification of inner conflict (Rom. 7:15-25) seems to get submerged by the brilliant persona he develops for Christians in his many letters. This, I believe, is unfortunate; people may romanticize about how wonderful it would be to be such a model Christian, but I am afraid that is all it would be—romantic fantasy.

The persona which is encouraged in the passages I have quoted above is for Christian folk in general. Those who aspire to be religious leaders are urged by Paul towards an even more elaborate persona (1 Tim. 3:2-7). By contrast, centuries after Paul's writings to Christians were completed, Martin Luther opened up a concept that added another dimension to the matter of persona and shadow—a dimension, I believe, of humanness and reality. Something like Saint John Chrysostom in the myth, Luther became terribly shaken celebrating his first mass. He, too, realized his great unworthiness and the tremendous unapproachableness of God. To describe the experience and the feeling, Luther used the word *Anfechtung*. There is no English equivalent for the word, but Luther variably described the experience as a trial sent by God to test him and an assault sent by the devil to destroy him. He declared it to be all the doubt, turmoil, panic, despair, and desolation that may invade a person.

Luther's struggles with *Anfechtungen* seem to have been a regular and integral part of his life. But whether his "attack" was mild or severe, he could find healing in reading the Psalms because to him they seemed to speak most clearly of and to *Anfechtung*.

After recovering from a particularly bad bout with depression in 1527, he concluded that intense upheavals of the spirit are necessary for valid solutions of spiritual problems. The emotional reactions of the experience may be unduly acute, but that is because the devil "always turns a louse into a camel." Whatever, the way of a man with God cannot be tranquil.

"If I live longer," he said, "I would like to write a book about *Anfechtungen,* for without them no man can understand Scripture, faith, the fear or the love of God. He does not know the meaning of hope who was never subject to temptations. David must have been plagued by a very fearful devil. He could not have such profound insights if he had not experienced great assaults."

The thesis of this book states that one moves toward wholeness and completeness *(teleios)* not only through the continued infusion of goodness and righteousness but also through the "owning" of one's shadow and the conscious incorporation of it into one's self; that I am indeed incomplete and inauthentic unless and until I begin this process. A persona is not a person; to believe it *is,* is to delude one's self.

But there is paradox present in this, just as there is in so much of Christianity. (Possibly Paul avoided it because of this—new converts do not need paradoxes; they need black and white ethics.) The paradox is simply that that which contains the potential for the greatest evil is at the same time *necessary* for attainment of the highest good, namely wholeness *(teleios)*. Jesus said, "You must be *teleios* (whole) as your Father in heaven is *teleios*."

There is risk involved in making friends with your shadow— that is true. However, for some people the risk lies in a kind of superstition that believes acknowledging something gives it power. Quite the contrary is, in fact, true. In most cases, *not* to acknowledge a thing is to give it power. People foolishly hesitate to go to the doctor because they are afraid the doctor will confirm what they suspect. They are afraid that going to the doctor will "make it happen"; doing nothing is safer. Meanwhile the disease gains more power. Friends and relatives foolishly cover and conceal a person's chemical dependency because they are afraid that confronting it will make it "be." They believe that if they don't say anything about it it really "isn't." Meanwhile everyone's refusal to acknowledge it simply gives it more power and enables the disease slowly to destroy the person.

Likewise, not to acknowledge the existence of your shadow because you believe to do so would give it power *is the very thing which will in fact give it power.* We saw in the last chapter how another, "alien" personality may take over a person's life, discarding completely all previous values. There are indeed dramatic cases where the unassimilated, denied, repressed shadow suddenly erupts and takes over, but even in less exaggerated ways, as we shall see, the unrecognized shadow may influence our lives significantly.

Frankly, Paul's way is easier than Jesus'; that is perhaps why so much of the Christian church has for so long seemed to identify in its teaching with Paul rather than with Jesus. Essentially Paul presses for a one-sided goodness; Jesus says "Be whole and complete." Maybe this is something of what he had in mind when he said, "Enter by the narrow gate; for the gate is wide and the way is easy, that leads to destruction, and those who enter by it are many. For the gate is narrow and the way is hard, that leads to life, and those who find it are few" (Matt. 7:13-14).

There can be no doubt that Jesus' way of life makes great demands on people for personal responsibility. Freedom in any form always does that. To become aware of one's self and to honestly face the duality in one's self can be very painful and disheartening. *This* is what the real risk is in turning and looking at your shadow. Luther's *Anfechtungen* literally immobilized him. Little wonder, then, that many of the followers of Jesus prefer the directives of Paul. Frankly it is much easier to be told what to do and what not to do—what is right and what is wrong, what is white and what is black—than to "work out your own salvation with fear and trembling" (Paul wrote that! —Phil. 2:12). Probably the masses of humanity could not handle Jesus' psychological ethic. Left to themselves to function on their own responsibility, most would undoubtedly fall into terrible sin, deny God, and wreck their lives. Most, we could argue, would not want an increased awareness of themselves; most perhaps would not know what to do with it if they ever achieved it. Therefore, better to map out their lives *for* them.

But we *are* dealing with freedom and that is what Jesus' position gives and Paul's position seems to deny. Freedom involving choice and possible conflict is at the root of our creation by God, so it is not surprising to find it running through everything Jesus said and did. But it is a violation of that freedom to erect a system of shoulds, oughts, and musts and to encourage repression of everything that contradicts that system in order to promote goodness, and it remains a violation no matter how glorious the goodness is which appears to be achieved.

6

SHADOW
and projection

I have learned that a very helpful element in counseling and teaching is to push things into the absurd. Generally speaking, plain, ordinary truth is only nominally impressive. But if I can find a way to take plain, ordinary truth and increase it to the 10th power, exaggerating it into the absurd or the ridiculous, then I can usually not only get my hearers' attention, but even help enable them to hear what I'm saying. Sometimes people are startled and may even complain about "overstatement," but I simply smile and say, "Yes, but when I say it *that* way, you don't miss the point, do you?"

Jesus used this technique fairly regularly in his teaching. One time he said,

> Why do you see the speck that is in your brother's eye, but do not notice the log that is in your own eye? Or how can you say to your brother, 'Brother, let me take out the speck that is in your eye,' when you yourself do not see the log that is in your own eye? You hypocrite, first take the log out of your own eye, and then you will see clearly to take out the speck that is in your brother's eye (Luke 6:41-42).

How ridiculously absurd! Can you even *imagine* the picture? It is impossible; it is fantastic; it is nonsensical. A person with a *log* stuck in his eye! Even if that were physically possible, he couldn't get close enough to another person to see whether that person had a *speck* in his eye or not!—let alone try to *take it out!* Oh, the whole thing is just utterly and absolutely preposterous!

And that is precisely the point. Yet that is precisely what many of us human beings dearly love to do: go around offering to take specks out of others' eyes when we can scarcely see through our own timber; go around offering to heal others when we are sick unto death with our own disease; go around offering to pick nits from others' garments when we are clothed in stinking, filthy, infested rags.

Although this is true, there is a very strong resistance within human beings to believe its truth. In the abstract we all know that we are not perfect ("After all no one is *perfect;* we all have our faults"), but in the concrete, substantial effort is required to recognize that we are less good than we like to imagine ourselves to be. We may walk away from the prayer of general confession on Sunday morning feeling rather good that our sins, whatever they have been or are, are indeed forgiven. But the amount of conscious effort made to determine specifically what those sins were or are, although it will certainly vary from person to person, generally speaking will be quite minimal. Public confession simply is not the place for one to face one's shadow in the concrete, and facing it any other way is not to face it at all. So while we may be conscious of Jesus' ridiculously absurd teaching, we may hear it only with our ears, and thus *not* hear it. Hearing it would mean coming to grips with our shadows (the logs in our eyes), and who really wants to do that?

It is no doubt clear by now that the shadow does not usually present a very pleasant sight. Because my shadow is the opposite of personal and collective ideals, it is largely negative and destructive, since personal and collective ideals tend towards the positive and constructive. Furthermore, my shadow is all that has been repressed for the sake of my ego-ideal. The rebellious, opposing nature of my shadow is particularly disruptive and painful to my ego, especially as my ego tries to fulfill the expectations and demands of my super-ego or conscience. My ego is prone to stand looking at my persona—my light and bright side which I parade before society. There is, frankly, little motivation for it to turn around and gaze upon my shadow. After all, we all know what happened to Pandora.

But my shadow refuses to be ignored; it agitates for expression. My ego would like very much to get rid of my shadow because of the power it has to embarrass me or get me into serious trouble with society. While my ego is standing, facing society, looking through my persona, my shadow is regularly poking it in the back saying, "Hey, hey, I'm here." And my ego, without turning around, keeps smiling at society through my persona, all the while elbowing my shadow into the background of my psyche and muttering to it out of the corner of its mouth, "Get back down there and shut up, you devil."

The shadow is obviously something we really don't want. But as Jung has said, "Mere suppression of the shadow is as little of a remedy as beheading would be for headache." What then? Well, when you have something that you really don't want, the easiest way to get rid of it is to throw it away. And that is precisely what often happens. We throw away or project away that undesirable stuff, but we throw it or project it *onto* other people or groups, things or events. Projection is an unconscious mechanism whereby we transfer psychic characteristics from ourselves to another person, group, object, or event. It is essentially a defense mechanism, designed to protect ourselves and preserve our security. Knowing ourselves may be threatening, and the more threatening it is the more likely a person is to project. It is a very common way of dealing with one's shadow, even though in actual fact projection is *not to deal with* your shadow at all. Projection, as we shall see, turns out to be self-deceptive and only harms the projectee as well as the projector.

Usually the recipients of projections are people or groups of people, although things and events get them too. Have you ever walked through a room, preoccupied with your thoughts, and tripped on the leg of a chair? And did you indignantly turn on the chair as though it were some great adversary and want to kick it good? That, of course, would not be acceptable for an adult (child, maybe; adult, no); so you settled for a mere verbal chastisement and muttered, "Stupid chair."

To an objective observer the event would appear quite humorous and your irrationality would be obvious. How, pray tell, can an inanimate object possess the quality of stupidity? It can't. But you may project your own stupidity onto it and be relieved. Not that you are a stupid person, but in all probability if you had paid closer attention to where you were walking and had not been so preoccupied, the accident would not have happened. Facing the reality of your clumsiness, however, may be a threat to your image of yourself, and so you throw it away; you get rid of the undesirable by projecting it on the chair and saying, "Stupid chair."

However, more projection is made onto people and groups of people than onto things. Parents, for instance, often project substantial shadow material onto their children because they are convenient scapegoats, readily at hand to "field the throw." In pathological family systems it is often possible to use this assumption to determine the character of the parents on the basis of the character and behavior of the adolescent child. The child *becomes* the shadow of the parents and acts it out. The adolescent *is* everything that the parents *are not*. Because the personas of such parents are generally very positive (respectable, righteous, and law-abiding), the shadow qualities which get projected onto their child are negative (disrespectfulness, unrighteousness, and rebellion). These qualities (projections) fielded or absorbed by the youngster become his persona. The child may reveal in a most terrible way the parents' secret shadow.

The tragedy of this pattern is that there is no awareness of it on the part of any of the people concerned. The parents may in fact be well-meaning people and simply cannot fathom why their child is as he is. (For instance, it used to be taken for granted that preachers' kids would be hellions. In some parsonage families this is still true.) To objective observers the reasons may be quite obvious. This, of course, is due to the fact that one's shadow is always much more evident to others than to oneself.

> Speak crossly to your little boy
> And smack him when he sneezes.
> He only does it to annoy
> Because he knows it teases.

This clever little nursery rhyme focuses on a common shadow projection, not only for parents of little boys, but for all people. "He does what he does just to annoy and upset me." It is, in fact, a favorite accusation of spouses to spouses. Marriage counselors regularly hear charges and countercharges which are nothing more than shadow projections. He can see her shadow (which is invisible to her) as well as she can see his (which is invisible to him). He gets angry with her for dumping on him her garbage, and she gets angry with him for dumping on her his garbage. "It's her fault." "No, it's his fault."

Failure to be "in touch" with our own shadow keeps us from the realization that behaviors, characteristics, or manners of other people which annoy us are probably projected material from our own unconscious. A clear illustration of this appears in another nursery rhyme which, as is often the case, appears to make little sense, but which actually identifies with a common experience.

> I do not love thee, Doctor Fell;
> The reason why I cannot tell.
> But this I know and know full well,
> I do not love thee, Doctor Fell.

Now I do not have the foggiest notion who Doctor Fell is, but that is neither here nor there. The thrust of the rhyme speaks to the experience of not liking someone but not knowing *why* you don't like him. If this has never happened to you, you are probably extremely self-aware and know your shadow intimately. For the rest of us it is not an uncommon experience.

Let's say you are introduced to a person by a mutual friend. After the encounter your friend says to you, "Well, what do you think of John?" You reply, "Well, John is OK. But, I don't know; there's just something about him that I don't like." And your friend asks, "Oh, what's that?" And you honestly reply, "I really don't know; I can't put my finger on it."

In this commonplace illustration what is probably happening is this: you are sensitive to an undesirable trait in John's personality which is also a part of your own personality. But because you are unconscious of it in yourself, you cannot clearly identify it in John. All you "know" is that there is something about him that is disturbing to you. If your friend should say to you, "I'll bet I know what it is you don't like; John comes off rather ingratiating," you may be surprised to feel an "aha!" experience in yourself and you may agree saying, "Yes. I'll bet that's it. How did you guess?" If your friend is honest and believes your relationship can stand it, he will reply quietly, "You tend to be ingratiating yourself."

As we shall see, this kind of honest feedback by people who know us is one of the best ways of learning what our shadow looks like, albeit probably the one which we resist most of all. You will probably turn to your friend and in irritation or mild anger say, "What do you mean by that? I'm not that way at all!" Such a response is a natural defense against a threat to your ego. Your friend is holding up a part of your shadow for you to see —something to which you had been blind before—and it is a scary and threatening experience. You may choose to preserve your image of yourself by continuing to employ the defense mechanism of denial, or you may choose to entertain the feedback of your friend with the idea that there might just be a shred or two of truth in it. The former is safer but will only serve to keep your blinders in place and maintain your current level of self-awareness (or unawareness). The latter is chancier and scarier but is one of the tasks involved in ultimately making friends with your shadow.

We do not ordinarily project shadow material willy-nilly; there is usually a peg or hook on which to hang the accusation. The projectee, or person receiving the projection, has something about him that makes the attachment of such an image possible. And that is what makes it all the more difficult for the projector to see his own participation in the qualities he is condemning in the projectee. Lucy may say of Martha, "But she *is* dishonest;

she was caught stealing from the bank where she works and was convicted. Why am I dishonest because I speak out against dishonesty and want to keep Martha from ever having contact again with public funds?"

However, if Lucy were to see herself honestly she would see in herself the dishonesty she abhors in Martha. She would see herself cheating her son out of the opportunity to develop as his own person because she needs to keep him dependent on her. She would see herself stealing from the supermarket when she sees herself longchanged by the cashier and rationalizes her theft saying, "They can afford it." She would see herself stealing from the integrity of every person who is the subject of her gossip.

In spite of conscious rejection, that which is being rejected may actually exercise secret fascination. True, George is *not* an unfaithful spouse and he *detests* infidelity in others, but does he perhaps have a secret desire to be unfaithful, a desire so morally repugnant that he must repress it?

Some years ago one of my married students in our hospital's program of clinical pastoral education appeared to be experiencing some difficulty in ministering to single women who had just delivered their babies (unwed mothers). Actually it was I who identified the "difficulty"; he was quite unaware of it. From the written accounts of his ministerial visits with the new mothers it appeared to me that he was initially unaccepting of them —not in any overt way, but more subtly, being cool, somewhat distant, not empathic as he was with other patients. In his conversations with them he seemed to want to lead them into a kind of "liturgy" wherein they would "confess" their premarital sexual activity and express their regrets about it. This was, of course, all very low-key and subtle, and in a similar fashion he would assure them of the grace and forgiveness of God. Once this experience had occurred in the relationships he was quite accepting and empathic towards the young women. If it did not occur the distance remained throughout the relationship.

When I brought this observation to his attention he was open enough to hear it and did not become defensive. However, he had no real understanding of the dynamics behind this behavior other than that he saw premarital sexual intercourse as a violation of God's law. "Yes," I said, "I understand that. But you minister to people who violate God's law in a variety of sins— I have read your written accounts. You don't relate to them as you relate to these young women. You don't encourage them into such a 'liturgy' as you do these young women."

One day in a supervisory hour together he and I were talking about his growing up experience. Quite innocently I asked him how he got along with girls as an adolescent. He smiled and said, "Real well."

"Ever 'mess around'?" I queried.

"Oh, no," he said.

"Ever want to?"

He looked at me and replied, "Well, sure; sure I did."

"But you never did."

"Right," he said, "I never did."

I decided to move along with him a little further and asked, "As you have looked back, have you ever wished that you had?"

"I don't know," he said, "I don't think I've ever really thought about it."

Then I said, "Has it ever occurred to you that those young unwed mothers have obviously *done* what you at their age very much *wanted to do, but didn't?*"

He sat without saying a word, letting it all soak in.

"How do you feel towards those young women?" I asked.

Quickly he answered, "I'm mad at them."

"Yes," I said, "but are you now aware of any other feeling that maybe even precedes your anger?"

There was no response. He just sat in his chair looking at me. Then suddenly a grin cracked on his face, and he began to laugh quietly. Still looking directly at me he said, "What do you know. I'm envious."

This man was a brave man. He allowed the insight to come. He didn't continue his repression or deny it once he saw it. This Christian pastor had remained faithful to his values through his youth and had not permitted himself premarital sexual intercourse. Now he was called upon to minister to young women who had not done that. But they *should* have, he thought. If *he* could do it (even though he *wanted* to do otherwise), why couldn't they? So he was angry with them because they were "bad"—they went and did what he wanted to do and didn't. But he was also envious of them for the very same reason. (Remember, the shadow is perhaps everything we would *like* to be, but don't dare.)

There is no denying the young women presented a "hook" for him to hang his projected shadow on. Yes, seeing them stirred old regrets that he hadn't acted out his sexual wants as they had; so they received the projection of his lust. They became the ones who had to be punished, so to speak, before he could accept them. They had to be punished because they were bad. Only the "badness" was his own "badness" which he had written off long before. Of course he would have liked to have "messed around"—that is the abstract, the general confession, the "nobody's perfect" admission. *But in the concrete lust looks quite different.* That is why I say this man was a brave man. The unwed mothers "hooked" his projection and they received the evaluation which belonged on himself. His courage lay in his willingness to end his projection and make friends with his shadow.

Certainly the shadow can be projected anywhere. I have already mentioned parent to child and spouse to spouse. The projections between husband and wife are particularly distressing and problematic when time has allowed them to solidify. Each spouse resolutely sees the other as responsible for all the difficulties and himself or herself as innocent. The more deficiencies a person can point out in his spouse, the more confirmed he may become in the opinion of his own virtue. This may lead to physical aggression—the need to physically *persuade* the spouse of one's own rightness and his or her wrongness. As in all projection, the more I am convinced of my own rightness, the more wrongness I will project onto and see in others. The blacker other people become, the more white will be my own whiteness.

Projections occur in groups of all sorts—churches, clubs, associations; in places of employment; even in casual encounters. Of course it is quite possible to disagree, even disagree adamantly, with people without having to be accused of projecting your shadow. It is quite possible to confront and critique without being identified as a kettle calling a skillet black. But when you feel a sort of burning in your chest, an awareness in yourself that someone ought to "pay," or a sensation that you would like to call a person a "dirty dog," a "brazen hussy," a "controlled psychopath," or some similarly caustic title, you can be rather sure that this is your shadow, and no good will come of it unless you stop and turn the ego around and find it in yourself before you start out after it in others.

The shadow may also be projected onto groups of people, even whole nations. Undoubtedly much racial hatred, prejudice toward minorities (and majorities), and international conflict is the direct result of shadow projection. Shadow projection causes a terrible distortion in personal and social relationships because it leads us to see in those groups or nations all the negativity or evil which we have not faced in ourselves, and our usual reaction is one of paranoid fear and hate.

The wars and rumors of war of which Jesus spoke, national and international scandal, and crime in general seem to provide scapegoats for all sorts of people. Nazi Germany projected its shadow onto the Jews, and America and its allies projected their shadows onto the Nazis, the Japanese, and Italy. As a nation we have been able to project our shadow onto Russia, Korea, Vietnam, Iran. All of those nations certainly provided America with "hooks" on which to hang our shadow. But we are, of all peoples, most deluded if we believe we as a nation are only persona and do not provide other nations with hooks on which to hang their shadows. We as a nation practice the worst kind of self-deception if we sincerely believe we are perpetually "innocent."

Any time we see "the enemy," we can be fairly certain that our own projected shadow is in there somewhere. Many years ago Walt Kelly had *Pogo,* his comic strip character, say, "We have met the enemy, and they are us." Watergate shocked and angered and depressed many American people, but it provided us with a scapegoat on which to project our shadow. "How terrible," people said. "*I* would never *think* of doing anything so *despicable!*"

The book and movie "The Exorcist" provided a return to an ancient scapegoat on which countless legions of shadow have been projected: demons. Centuries ago St. Peter wrote, "Your adversary the devil prowls around like a roaring lion, seeking someone to devour." If we can project our own evil onto spirits or entities or the personification of evil *out there* somewhere then we may be free of responsibility and we may the more easily keep our whiteness white. It is very interesting to note that in the myths of old, the dragons, sphinxes, and beasts (projections of aggression, violence, and evil) always resided *outside* the gates of the city.

To the extent that I have to be right and good, *he, she, they,* or *it* will become the carrier of all the evil, real and potential, which I do not acknowledge within myself. If I do not face my inner enemy, it is inevitable that I will be driven to create an enemy outside.

Once again I am indebted to Heinrich Zimmer for recounting a tale out of *The Arabian Nights* which speaks so poignantly to the matter of projection—throwing away the undesirable. The title of the tale is "Abu Kasem's Slippers," and I retell it as follows:

Once upon a time in the city of Bagdad there lived a very famous and wealthy miser by the name of Abu Kasem. Interestingly enough Abu Kasem's claim to fame resided not so much in his person or his accomplishments, but of all things in the condition of his shoes. They were an absolute disgrace. Outrageous! They were so tattered and patched, repaired beyond repair, shingled with bits and pieces—even the motliest beggar in town would have been mortified to be caught dead in them. Children made jokes about them; people of the city claimed they were the only slippers he had ever owned. Even a benediction of sorts grew out of this phenomenon: "May your luck last as long as the slippers of Abu Kasem."

One day this celebrated businessman in his preposterous slippers went shuffling through the bazaar searching, as was his custom, for unusual bargains. One of the sellers of glass called him over and told him of an extraordinary buy on little crystal bottles. "Buy them, and I can sell them again for you at twice the price." Abu Kasem bought. A little later, with a bankrupt perfume merchant, he closed an exceptional deal on sweet rose water. Delighted with his business achievements Abu Kasem went home, poured the rose water into the fine crystal bottles, and set them high up on a shelf at the back of his house where they would be safe until he sold them.

Abu Kasem was well pleased with his morning and so decided to visit the House of the Baths. In the dressing room he met an acquaintance and fellow businessman, Omar ben Adi. "Abu Kasem," he said, as his glance fell on the wretched slippers, "I have great concern about you being the laughing-stock of the city. Such a clever businessman as you should certainly be able to afford a decent pair of slippers." Abu Kasem attentively studied one of the monstrosities and said to his friend, "I have been thinking about that very matter for many years, but actually there is still good use in them." Omar ben Adi shook his head, and that was the end of the conversation.

When Abu Kasem finished his bath he returned to the dressing room and put on his long gown. He reached for his slippers but they were not there. Somehow they had been pushed under the bench and where his old slippers had been was a different pair—beautiful and apparently brand new. "No doubt Omar ben Adi bought them for me while I was in the bath," thought Abu Kasem. "What a marvelous surprise!" With great satisfaction he pulled on the slippers and went home.

But of course this is not at all what had happened. Omar ben Adi had not generously provided the miserly Abu Kasem with a new pair of slippers. They were the brand new slippers of the cadi of Bagdad, a judge of the city.

Like Abu Kasem, the judge had come to wash at the House of the Baths. He had undressed and left his slippers at the bench. But upon returning to the dressing room he could not find his slippers, and he was furious. The bath men looked and looked but could only come up with a pair of wretched objects which *everyone* immediately recognized as the infamous footwear of Abu Kasem. The judge went into a rage. "Not only is he a miser, he is a thief and he shall be punished!"

The cadi's servants took the tattered slippers and went to

Abu Kasem's house where, of course, they found him wearing the new slippers of the judge. The judge locked him up, and it cost Abu Kasem a pretty penny to get himself free because the court knew as well as everyone else in Bagdad how rich he really was. He tried to explain that it was all a mistake—but in vain. Besides, the truth *was* rather silly.

Sad, sorry, and angry, Abu Kasem decided to get rid of the things that had caused him so much trouble and cost him so much money. With a fury he threw them into the Tigris River and declared that that was that!

The next day a fisherman's net brought the slippers back out of the river. The fisherman of course recognized the slippers as those of Abu Kasem and took them to his house in the hope of receiving a reward from the rich man. No one was at home when he arrived—the doors were tightly shut—so he threw the slippers in through an open window high up on the back of the house, expecting to come back later to claim a reward.

The slippers landed perfectly in the middle of the shelf where Abu Kasem had stored his fine crystal bottles of rose water and the entire collection was swept to the floor and lay there, a soggy mass of glassy fragments mixed with perfumed mud.

Abu Kasem's grief was almost overwhelming when he discovered the tragedy. He beat his head against the wall, crying, "Those miserable, wretched slippers. I will get rid of them once and for all!" He took a shovel and went quickly into the garden and began to dig a hole there in order to bury the things. But as fate would have it, his next-door neighbor, who was always interested in what went on at Abu Kasem's house, happened to see him. He said to himself, "That old codger has servants enough to dig holes; why is he out there digging himself? Aha!" deduced the neighbor, "He has a treasure buried there." So off he went to the cadi and informed against Abu Kasem's violation of the law—for according to the law, the earth and all that is hidden in it is the property of the ruler; treasure seekers' finds belong to the caliph.

Abu Kasem was swiftly called before the judge. As he tried to explain that he had only dug up the earth to bury an old pair of slippers, everyone in the court laughed uproariously. The more he spoke, the guiltier he sounded. The fine which the judge finally imposed on Abu Kasem was so great his heart nearly stopped.

Now he was desperate. He would throw the cursed slippers into the sewer where no fisherman's net would retrieve them and where they would be carried away through the big pipe never to trouble him again.

But it was not to be. The slippers stopped up the sewer. The dirty water ran out all over the street. A terrible stench accompanied the flooding and the residents of the area complained. The workmen cleaned out the sewer and uncovered Abu Kasem's slippers. And he was once again before the cadi.

In order to get out of jail this time Abu Kasem had to pay more dinars than the sum total of all his previous fines. But now would be the end of the slippers. He decided to burn them. They were still wet from the sewer so he put them out on his balcony to dry. A dog on the balcony next door was attracted by the strong sewer smell of the funny looking objects and jumped over to snatch one. But while playing with them the dog dropped one and it fell to the street below. Unfortunately a woman was passing by at the precise moment and the slipper struck her directly on the top of her head. Also unfortunately, she happened to be pregnant, and the shock and force of the blow brought on a miscarriage. The woman's husband hauled Abu Kasem into court and demanded damages.

The rich miser's wealth was now reduced to nothing. The rich miser himself was a broken man. But before he left the court he faced the judge and made an earnest plea. As he held the slippers aloft the sight was so amusing the judge began to laugh. And when he made his plea, the judge laughed all the more. "My lord," he said, "these slippers are the cause of all my agony and suffering. They have bankrupted me of money and spirit. I therefore ask you to declare that I shall never again be held responsible for the evil which they will surely bring upon me."

With that the tale of Abu Kasem's slippers ends, only to be followed by this moral: The cadi could not reject his plea. And Abu Kasem learned, at tremendous cost, how evil can come out of not changing slippers often enough.

Well, now, isn't that a rather disappointing moral? Is that all that is to be gained from this tragi-comedy of Abu Kasem? Have we been led through the drama of one man's life only to conclude that he had trouble because he didn't change his slippers?

No. "Abu Kasem's Slippers" is a marvelous illustration of the fact that you cannot get rid of your shadow by throwing it away. Projecting the shadow onto others does not free you of it, but only causes harm to others and certainly to yourself. You may work diligently and expend passionate energy, but in the end projection bankrupts you. Abu Kasem's continued effort to get rid of his slippers—his avaricious shadow—only grew and snowballed in destruction, finally almost burying him. The only salvation was to admit to their being the cause of his troubles; his shadow was ruining his life.

The more you try simply to dispose of the old man or woman the more tenaciously he or she will hang on. You may try to stomp on it, bury it, drown it, whatever your image; but it will not give up. Nor can you simply take off the old, throw it away, and put on the new in a once-and-for-all kind of move, confidently or smugly saying, "That is that."

Abu Kasem almost reached his end (but not quite) before he

finally realized that he could not get rid of his slippers by throwing them away. In despair he pleaded with the judge not to hold him responsible for any future deviltries the slippers might play. But the judge only laughed at his nonsensical attempt to evade responsibility. Again, which is easier to say—"It wasn't I; it was those cursed slippers!" or "I am innocent; it was my demon made me do it."

Abu Kasem never got rid of his slippers, but he did win. The tale says that in the end the judge could not refuse his request. *He was given release, but the final release would have to come from within him.*

God in his goodness has released us from the power of our own evil. But the final release must lie in our decision to face that evil and win. If we try simply to throw it away by projecting it outside, our shadow will only laugh at our impotent foolishness, and bring pain, agony, and even destruction to others and to ourselves.

7

SHADOW
and control

Robert Louis Stevenson wrote a fascinating account of ego and shadow in his story *Dr. Jekyll and Mr. Hyde.* Essentially the story deals with an exceptionally worthy and benevolent doctor who invented a compound or potion which would enable him to turn into his opposite. This, he believed, would give him the opportunity to enjoy the pleasures which he found himself unable "to reconcile with his imperious desire to carry his head high and wear a more than commonly grave countenance before the public."

Initially these "pleasures" were merely undignified and worldly, but Mr. Hyde, Dr. Jekyll's counterpart, became more and more purely evil and eventually did not stop even at murder. The change at first was entirely voluntary, but at the end the personality of Dr. Jekyll was completely enveloped by Mr. Hyde.

Dr. Jekyll and Mr. Hyde presents us with a reasonable rationale for avoiding the shadow. I can recall my aunt telling me as a little boy, "Play with fire and you'll get burned." Another adage says, "Court the devil and pay for it." Turning around from the persona and looking into that shadow can indeed be overwhelming—and for many that is reason enough not to do it.

I have had the opportunity to address a great number of groups of people, many of them Christian church groups. When I have talked with them about the shadow, I have regularly asked them a very personal question: "Given the proper circumstances (whatever that might mean) do you believe you would be capable of willfully destroying the life of another human being?"

Without exception people hedge by demanding to know what I mean by "the proper circumstances," but I honestly reply that that really is irrelevant, and besides, I don't even know what I mean by it myself. I simply repeat the question and urge them to deal with the basic issue of whether they believe they have within themselves the potential for murder.

When I have asked for a show of hands, usually some people raise their hands for neither yes nor no. They are perhaps undecided—or afraid. Generally the yeses have greatly outnumbered the nos; however, in every group there have invariably been some nos. Some of these people earnestly believe that they *cannot kill;* others are afraid that if they *say* they can do it, they *will* do it.

It should be clear by this point in our investigation that the shadow does exist, and that denying, repressing, or projecting it does no good for a person whatsoever. That which is unconscious cannot be dealt with. And unless one deals with his shadow, he is at its mercy. We have already seen illustrations of the shadow breaking through and overcoming the "innocent," and we have seen the catastrophe it brought about because the innocent had no control over it. The reason why the innocent had no control over it was that he or she believed it didn't exist.

If a person believes that to be angry is sinful and, consequently, unacceptable, he will repress his anger and deny he ever feels any. He may be on the verge of rage, but will honestly believe that he is not angry and will tell you so if you ask him.

The great risk involved in denying the shadow is very evident to anyone observing such a phenomenon. It is then that you begin to realize how powerful the mechanism of denial is. But when you observe the shadow breaking through that person's defenses as though the defenses were toothpicks before an avalanche, you become convinced that there is *no* match for the repressed shadow which has grown into a giant.

Mark Johnson was reared in the atmosphere of a "religious" home. The dominant feature of the home's religion was piety. Piety, according to Mark's mother and father, was sweetness and faith, which excluded any and all expressions of anger, hostility, resentment, and, of course, conflict. Likewise human sexuality had no place in family conversations because such talk was inappropriate to a godly family. All anger and anything hinting of sexuality had to be, and was, repressed. Mark, along with the other members of the family, succeeded admirably in keeping the home free of hostile expressions and angry confrontations. But not without paying a rather expensive price: three members of the family fell ill emotionally, the repressed feelings having taken their toll within the psyches of the victims.

When Mark later left the restrictive atmosphere of the home to attend a university, he began to unlearn some of his well-learned behavior patterns and felt good about his "liberation" from the old taboos about anger and sex. But it was an intellectual exercise at most, because when Mark married and moved into a new close family relationship, the old taboos rose from the grave and came back to Mark full of life. He could not stand the normal conflicts which naturally occurred in his relationship with his wife. He tried persuading her to take up his newly resurrected taboos on expressed anger, but she refused. He tried avoiding his anger by walking out on the conflict, but this of course resolved nothing.

In time his efforts to maintain a persona of sweetness and faith at the price of suppressing and denying shadow anger and rage proved to be more than his psyche was willing to pay. In the midst of a quarrel one evening he left his wife, got into his car, drove onto a freeway, and raced down the highway at breakneck speed with no destination in mind except ultimate self-destruction. When he returned home exhausted he was in a semidaze and told his wife he was sorry, he didn't know what came over him.

Shadow rage continued to break through in varying degrees. Twice he verbally threatened suicide. Once in the midst of a quarrel he beat his wife severely. On another occasion he threw a chair through a window in his home. Each time he appeared to be possessed with rage, according to his wife, and each time he apologized to her afterward, saying, "I don't know what came over me."

Mark entered therapy at his wife's urging and in time realized his shadow was indeed a part of him and had to be dealt with consciously. He became convinced that trying to destroy it would only destroy him and possibly others. As long as he avoided it or gave it casual recognition (as in his university days) he had no control over it; the bit was in *his* mouth and the shadow held the reins. But once he faced it, willing to risk looking at his own evil and potential evil, he was into the process of making friends with his shadow. The old adage, "Let sleeping dogs lie," may be good advice provided the sleeping dogs *never* wake up. But that seems a little unreasonable to expect. It would be much more realistic to come to terms with your shadow *before* it breaks through—before the rampaging dogs wreak havoc.

Sheldon Kopp, in his book *If You Meet the Buddha on the Road, Kill Him!* (Science and Behavior, 1972), says,

I abhor the social institution of slavery, would not participate in it, and am ready to put myself on the line politically to eradicate it. And yet in the secret darkness of my savage heart, I know that I would dig owning slaves. It would be wildly exciting to own another human being, to completely control his destiny, to do what I wished with and to him, to completely have my way with him. I would play out my every self-centered whim on such a hapless object without regard to anyone's pleasure but my own. I like the fact that I can enjoy indulging in such fantasies, not only because of the immediate satisfaction that they afford, but because of the way in which they increase my freedom to live decently. By recognizing this evil in myself, and by satisfying it in fantasy, I decrease the possibilities that I will find some devious ways of living it out with other people. Because I do not pretend that I have no wish to control and degrade another human being, I come to own those wishes, and to be in a position never to express them except by conscious, deliberate and responsible choice. As a result, I am usually free of the temptation to try to manipulate and control others surreptitiously.

One of my own favorite fantasies is that of destroying villains with dynamite. The subject of these fantasies (the villain) is usually an entity which I cannot confront; for example, the tax-makers or a computer or a recorded telephone message. Or the villain is a chain of buck-passers in which no link will assume responsibility; for example, department stores, building contractors, and the federal government. Or it is a person in a passing or momentary situation which is not likely to be repeated by the same person; for example, a motorist who cuts sharply in front of me in the midst of heavy traffic or a driver who pulls in front of me into the last available parking place in the lot and is out of his car and gone before I can even blow my horn.

In my fantasy I go back to my memories of the Western movies of the '40s and I use the old plunger-type box which the "bad guys" used to blow up the stage to get the money box. I run the wires from the box to the dynamite charge which I place under the villain, and with satanic glee I plunge down the handle of the device with both hands and blow the bugger to smithereens.

Kopp says, "By recognizing this evil in myself, and by satisfying it in fantasy, I decrease the possibilities that I will find some devious ways of living it out with other people." I allow myself to do what I do in my fantasy because I believe that I will not allow myself to do it in reality. Granted, this fantasy does not resolve any of the issues raised by the above situations, but it controls my shadow rage which comes vividly to life when I am intimidated or abused in such situations. I would be a liar and a fool were I, in those situations, to say, "Oh, well, it's really nothing." Were I to do that consistently and repeatedly I would one day find myself writing hateful and threatening letters to government officials, catching up with the rude motorist on the highway and running him off the road, or slashing the tires of the scab who steals the last parking spot. I *could* do any of those things. Knowing that I could—that I have the potential within me to do them—allows me the control that I will never have if I continue to say to myself and others, "Oh, I could never do that."

Several years ago a young woman resident of a small town near where I live was picked up while hitchhiking and raped by the driver of the car. By the time she managed to get home she was hysterical. Her father notified the police immediately and medical tests were conducted. Two sheriff's detectives and the young victim, along with her father, retraced the route to the place of the alleged rape. After a sleepless night, the young woman's father started out on his own investigation. He had his daughter's fairly complete description of the man and the car and he began talking to people and asking questions. Soon he had a name for the man whose person and automobile fit the description given by his daughter. He went to the neighborhood where the man was reported to live, asked the mailman for the precise house, and pulled up in front of it. Later, in a newspaper interview, he shared his feelings of that moment:

> After I was pretty sure I had the right guy I kind of thought I ought to sit outside his house and plug him with a deer rifle. Those are pretty un-Christian thoughts, but I had them.
>
> Then common sense tells you you've got a wife and five kids, and they need you. And I'm sure the man needs some kind of treatment. But I feel he certainly can't be allowed to run loose in society.

This father presents a striking contrast to those who believe that a personal evil once owned will be acted out. Not so! We can do nothing about the feelings, the urges, the drives that come to us, but we can do everything about what we *do* with them. Luther once said we cannot prevent the birds of the air from flying over our heads; but we *can* prevent them from building a nest in our hair. Keeping them from building nests in our hair, however, requires *work*—control and discipline.

The one condition that many people find more painful than facing their shadow is that of bearing the pressure of an urge and suffering the frustration or pain of refusing to satisfy it. No doubt it would have been satisfying and justifiable to that father to pull the trigger on his deer rifle and "plug" the man who raped his daughter. Sweet revenge! The birds flew over his head alright, and it took some shooing to keep them from building a nest. But "then common sense tells you. . . ."

In order to avoid the rigors of dealing with these urges and drives when they experience them, some people would rather not acknowledge them and convince themselves that they are not there. The father could have said, "I am a Christian man. Christians are supposed to love their enemies and do good to those who do them evil. Therefore I have no inkling of wanting to do this man in." That would appear noble and commendable, as well as a lot less painful than disciplining oneself to deal with the temptation to murder. Repression always appears less painful than discipline and control; unfortunately it is also more dangerous because it *causes us to act without consciousness of motive*— hence, irresponsibly. Consciousness allows a person to act responsibly; discipline and control enable him to choose to do so.

Freedom and personal responsibility go hand in hand. If I am to enjoy the freedom of will given me by my Creator I will recognize the need for responsible behavior and I will opt for that. Maturity helps a person realize that responsible behavior often demands self-discipline and self-control. Acknowledging the shadow does not thereby absolve one of responsibility for it. Personal responsibility is to say, "I choose to do this because as a responsible person I *want* to do it." This is quite different from the usual, "I really ought to . . . ," "Actually I should . . . ," "I had better . . . ," or "I must. . . ." These all seem to indicate a motivation from without, and usually this is true. Whenever I say, "Actually I should . . ." chances are very great that I really *don't* want to, I feel some external pressure to, there are possible or real rewards if I do, or there are possible or real negative consequences if I don't. Even in authentic personal responsibility when I say "I choose to do this because I want to do it," I still may very well *not* want to do it. That is to suffer the shadow. And I will not *always* win, but I make the struggle.

I believe that realization of personal responsibility is the key to self-control and self-discipline. In their book *Behavior Change Through Self-Control* (Holt, Rinehart & Winston, 1973), Marvin Goldfried and Michael Merbaum define self-control as "a personal decision arrived at through conscious deliberation for the purpose of instigating action which is designed to achieve certain desired outcomes or goals as determined by the individual himself."

This somewhat technical and complex definition indicates several points pertinent to our concern. For one thing, the self-controlled person himself determines what it is he will accomplish. It is not what is "expected" of me, or what the gang wants, or what the pastor of the church wants, or what is "patriotic," or what Mom wants. This is my own; this is what *I* will do.

Also, he may have to make conscious and deliberate adjustments in his life or environment in order to accomplish what he wills. This is a common aspect of self-discipline. Insight alone is not curative. Change—action—is involved. Recognizing avarice in my shadow and owning it as a real part of me is excellent growth movement. But alone it will do nothing to heal my marriage which is going to pieces because I work two jobs to make more money which I really don't need to live comfortably.

Another observation is that the person does not necessarily achieve self-control across the board. Because I have disciplined myself in dealing with my avaricious shadow it does not necessarily follow that I have self-control in experiencing my rage.

It is also evident in this definition that self-control is learned. It is not a gift that some are given and some denied. Some remarkable strides are being made in helping child-abusive parents and wife-abusive husbands learn self-control. Saying "I can't help it" seems to be a cop-out on personal responsibility. Again, it is, "What do I *want?*"

I have found that I can facilitate the struggle toward self-control by talking to myself, by talking to God, and by talking to others about what I am about. The next chapters will touch on talking with others, so here we focus on talking to God and talking to one's self.

Talking to yourself is for some people a questionable practice. I have found it, however, to be a very effective aid in self-discipline and the development of self-control. I have already mentioned my practice of fantasizing. Beyond that, I regularly talk to myself in private, sometimes carrying on substantial conversations. I do this at home, outdoors, in my car, and in my office. I do it at any time and for as short or long a period as is feasible or necessary. I support myself, challenge myself, confront myself, reward myself, laugh at myself, chastise myself, argue with myself, prod myself, provoke myself, and commend myself. I am sometimes startled by the objectivity I generate in these conversations; before I cultivated this habit I would have said that such objectivity was impossible.

Furthermore, amazingly enough, most of the time I listen. When I talk to myself, I listen to me. When I say, "OK, Bill, slow down," I relax. When I say, "Let's get with it," I abandon my sloth. When I say, "Who are you trying to kid?" I become authentic. And so it goes. Simply because I say to myself, "Don't do it" or "Let's do it," does not necessarily mean that I won't do it or that I will. But I have found that saying it helps me. And frankly I will take all the help I can get in this task of developing self-discipline.

I talk with God in much the same manner as I talk with myself. At some point many years ago I abandoned what I would call the formality of prayer. I implore, I beg, I thank, I complain, I compliment, I question, I plead. I am respectful, I am mundane, I am timid, I am profane, I am bold, I am confident.

I remember a seminary professor of mine saying, "Now, boys,

don't get too chummy with the Almighty." But why shouldn't we? God loves me, and I love God. We are certainly in this business together—this business of dealing with my own incarnate evil. What was it Jesus prayed? "Our Father . . . deliver us from evil."

God *will* do it. But we have to live with the shadow; indeed we are incomplete without it. We have to suffer it; indeed we will. We have to bridle *it* and take the reins, and *that* is a life's work.

8

SHADOW
and discovery

As usual Carol Bryce was on time for her appointment. Even
though it was only 7:30 A.M. she was bright, alert, and ready to
take on the day. At least that was the way she appeared. Carol
preferred early morning appointments because she did not feel
comfortable taking time away from her job, and this way she
could meet with me before starting her workday.

We had met together for several months and over that period
I had come to know Carol as a sensitive, conscientious, and interesting person. She was a physically attractive woman of 38,
single, had never been married. She was always well groomed,
and dressed to accentuate her natural beauty.

She had moved to Minneapolis some months before coming
to see me so that she might, she said, be closer to her mother
who was "getting up in years." That was partially true, but
Carol had also left the western town where she had lived and
worked for several years because she felt herself falling in love
with a married man and decided the best way to deal with that
situation was to leave it.

Carol told me she had experienced no real desire for lasting
male companionship or for marriage, home, and family. She

had sublimated her sexual urges and focused her energies on the development of her career as a teacher which she identified as being fulfilling and rewarding. But, she said, at this point in her life she was becoming aware of needs and desires, changes in attitudes, reassessments of values—"rumblings within" which were disturbing her tranquil life. The relationship with the married man had both frightened and excited her; it took her by surprise and that concerned her. After thinking through the ramifications of that relationship she decided to leave, move to Minneapolis, and take a job as a private secretary.

She first came to me complaining of vague dissatisfaction with her job, the new city, her roommate; time as always was moving on and she seemed to be standing still. She was not satisfied with herself or her life; it seemed to be slipping away from her much too quickly. She was much more interested in male companionship than she had ever been before, but felt rather "out of it" in terms of how to relate to men. She came wanting an opportunity to explore what was going on in her life and what some possible paths into the future might be. She was dissatisfied and wanted to do something about it.

Her story was really quite complicated, but a significant aspect of her growing up process was that her home environment was one that fostered suppression and repression of feelings. It was a religious atmosphere, quite genuine and nonjudgmental, but to please her parents Carol had masked her feelings with a consistent neutral pleasantness. That was why when she would appear at my office promptly at 7:30 A.M. for her appointment she would consistently appear bright, alert, and ready to take on the day, regardless of how she felt inside.

In the course of our meeting together Carol began to look more closely at the "rumblings" she had been experiencing in her inner self. In her exploration she bumped into some severe anger for having been underpaid for many years as a teacher and having played the role of the martyr. Then she brushed past avarice and discovered lust. But these things couldn't be there—she was a Christian woman and they were all contrary to what she believed herself to be. We talked about the persona and the shadow, the repression she had achieved for so many years, the ability to mask true feelings and play an "acceptable" role, and how at this point in her life the dark sister was beginning to clamor for equal time. Intellectually it all made sense, but it was more than she was willing to accept emotionally. Becoming aware of her other side seemed to excite her, but she resisted any kind of befriending it.

On this particular morning she seemed to want to get "right to it" as she sat down. "I had a dream last night," she said in a somewhat staccato voice. "It was scary, but I think I did the right thing."

"Sounds interesting," I said. "Tell me about it."

"I was in a hotel ballroom," she said, "one of those old types where there is a high ceiling and a sort of balcony running all around the big room. There were a lot of metal chairs set up at random throughout the ballroom, but I was the only person in the room. I went under the balcony at one end of the hall and saw a big mirror almost covering the end wall. I saw a reflection in the mirror; I don't know, I guess it was my own image, but I guess it wasn't either. It was all black and scary like a witch. I really couldn't clearly make it out. All I know is, when I saw it I was frightened and I slowly backed away. But I bumped into the chairs and turned my back on the mirror to move the chairs out of the way. When I turned around again the image had stepped out of the mirror and was slowly moving toward me. I kept backing away and the image kept coming. It didn't seem to be chasing me, just coming toward me. But I still couldn't clearly make it out. I turned around and started to run, knocking chairs over and throwing them behind me to block the way. I turned around and looked and the image was just going through the chairs, but it was a solid thing. I was very frightened and ran almost the length of the ballroom. Then I stopped in a little clearing of the chairs and I turned around and stood there facing the image. It was just two dimensional; I could see it was flat like a poster. I stooped down and started to roll it up from the floor, sort of like a roll of wallpaper. I rolled it up into a tube and lit a match and set fire to the end of the tube and held it while it burned up."

"And that was the end of the dream?" I asked.

"Yes," she said. "I woke up and I thought about it, and I think I did the right thing, don't you?"

"What do you mean," I said, "you think you did the right thing?"

"I destroyed it. I know what it was, and I destroyed it."

After a moment I asked, "Do you know why you destroyed it?"

"Of course," she said. "I was afraid of what it might do to me." Then she waited, and when I didn't respond, she said, "Well, what do you think?"

"I have a suspicion," I finally answered, "that you didn't destroy it at all, but like a phoenix it will rise again out of the ashes."

Make no mistake—looking into your own shadow is no Sunday afternoon picnic in the park. It is exciting, but it is scary. It takes nerve, determined nerve, not to flinch at the sight or be shocked or terrified by the image of one's shadow. It takes courage to stop projecting and accept responsibility for one's own inferior and evil self. Jung has said,

The shadow is a moral problem that challenges the whole ego-personality, for no one can become conscious of the shadow without considerable moral effort. To become conscious of it involves recognizing ·the dark aspects of the personality as present and real. This act is the essential condition for any kind of self-knowledge, and it therefore, as a rule, meets with considerable resistance.

Carol Bryce was not at all unusual in her resistance toward owning her shadow side. She simply did not want to believe that she could be other than she believed herself to be. But it is not until we see ourselves as we truly are instead of as we hopefully assume or wish we are that we can make any movement toward wholeness and completeness. Carol felt increasingly incomplete. *But she was not ready to believe that that which would help her towards completeness was that which she held to be undesirable, offensive, and certainly frightening.* Best get rid of it—so she tried doing that, even in her dream.

To discuss making friends with your shadow is one thing; to do it is quite something else. Imagine drawing your mouth together and gathering a pool of saliva. Now gently spit that pool of saliva into a drinking glass. Then do it again, and continue to do it until you have accumulated, say, half an inch of your saliva in the glass. Now look at it, study it, contemplate it—and then drink it.

Most of us have the same type of reaction to our shadow—the very thought of this is repulsive. It is truly my own; it is a part of me. But drink my saliva! Make friends with my shadow! Yech! Get rid of it!

Seeking to get rid of the shadow is certainly one way of dealing with it. But as we have seen, this means only repression and projection. That is why I said to Carol her "annihilation" of her shadow was only temporary; it certainly would resurrect and incarnate. Continued repression only gives more power to the shadow. Our projections transform the world we experience into a string of frames showing us our own pictures—our own faces —only we do not recognize them as our own. As repression and projection continue we can become increasingly isolated from the world we experience; instead of relating to it out of authentic humanness and reality of personality, we relate only through an illusion—a persona, a mask. And the world we experience is not the world as it is, but the wicked, evil world which our shadow projections produce.

Another possible way of dealing with the shadow is simply to let it have its own way—to act out the darkness, to assume no responsibility for what it does, but secretly or not so secretly to enjoy its mischief. Some people who do this like to claim that they are free agents, liberated from the inhibitions and taboos of a repressive society. They "let it all hang out." They are "ultimately aware" (whatever that means). But this is demonic. It is a rationalization for license. Such people range in their behavior from social boors to Hitlers. The end result of this way of dealing with the shadow is always destructive.

Neither of these ways of dealing with the shadow is constructive because both are one-sided and tend to cause a dissociation between conscious good and unconscious evil. Too much morality and too little morality are both antithetical to the Christian concept of wholeness and completeness.

The third possible way of dealing with the shadow is contained in the thesis of this book: Accept it and take its existence into account; learn its qualities and intentions; realize that in its ambiguity and paradox it is to be "suffered" and used constructively.

To each of you setting out on this journey, this pilgrimage

into the shadow, on to wholeness, I sincerely and strongly suggest *engaging a traveling companion to accompany you along the way*. Let this person be a friend—a trusted friend who will be able to understand your endeavor and who will accept and support you in it. This companion may be a professional counselor/therapist or not. That is not nearly as important as your companion being a person with whom you can feel confident; one whom you can trust. Let this be a person who will neither condemn you, scorn you, nor excuse you. Let this person be nonjudgmental and empathic. Negotiate with your companion an arrangement whereby you can "talk through" your progress with him or her as you proceed along your journey, sharing your growing awareness, asking for objective assessment (another's opinion) of your insights.

Not only is it a good feeling to be aware of the presence of a trusted friend on an exciting but scary journey, it is also advantageous to your goal achievement. Your dark side will become more real when it is exposed to another person—one who "knows" you. As we shall see, this is one of the most effective ways of learning what your shadow looks like.

Furthermore, the traveling companion provides an image of solidarity and security as you make your pilgrimage. This is important because encountering the shadow always means a certain amount of dissociation of ego and shadow; you, though you are one, tend to become two. When we look honestly at our dark side we sometimes lose confidence in our light side. This is natural and need not be alarming. Having a shadow in no way cancels our good qualities. Doubts may come, and on the journey we may become uncertain as to how life is to be lived. We may resolve one issue only to find two more in its place. This can be discouraging and depressing. But we can be confident that we will come together after we have come apart. This is the process towards wholeness.

Thus it is well to have a traveling companion who carries the projection of inner unity—of wholeness—so we may look to him or her for support and assurance when we feel "divided" within ourselves.

Insight has frequently been described as an "Aha!" moment. In becoming acquainted with our shadow it is more often an "Oh, no!" moment. Once at a conference a woman told me that she was quite sure she did not have a shadow side. It was a Sunday afternoon in midwinter and we were talking during a coffee break. A man who apparently was her husband came up to us, excused himself, and said to her, "I'm going to leave now; I'll see you at home."

He left and she said to me, "That's my husband." Then with mouth slightly turned down she added, "He's going home to watch the football game."

"You sound a little disgruntled," I said.

"Well, I certainly think he could gain more from this conference than from watching a football game. Sometimes I think he's addicted to it."

"It's that bad?" I said.

"Oh, at mealtimes it's impossible," she complained. "I call him and call him, and go into the den and just about have to physically drag him away from that tube. And all he says is, 'One more play; just one more play.'"

"Gee," I said, "that must be maddening."

There were sparks in her eyes as she said to me in quiet, deliberate phrases, "Sometimes I would like to go into that den, take that can of beer out of his hand, pour it over his head, and *crunch* the can on his miserable skull!"

"Well," I said, "for a woman who has no shadow, you certainly seem to be in touch with yours."

I realize that what I said to her was not all that "nice." But I consciously decided to let *my* shadow have a fling and I embarrassed her. She turned scarlet almost immediately and looked at me as though I had just caught her with her hand in the jam jar. Her insight was not an "Aha!"; it was a definite "Oh, no!" Nevertheless, there *was* insight.

There are a number of ways of getting acquainted with your shadow. One of the most valid and valuable is to listen to feedback from people who are close to us and know us. It is often the case that the shadow to which we are blind is blatantly visible to others; they can clearly see the qualities which are totally invisible to us. Spouses, children, and close friends, colleagues and work associates are usually the best sources of feedback, but are at the same time the most difficult to listen to. Our children are especially good resources because they are generally frank and open and are not governed by adult "propriety." In our more honest moments we believe these people are sincere in telling us (reporting back to us) how we come across, how we behave, how we appear; but we tend to discount their feedback saying that they are only projecting, or they have an axe to grind, or "Look who's calling *me* manipulative!" Listening to someone report on the shadow qualities they have observed in you can be rather threatening to your ego and can consequently arouse considerable defensiveness.

Driving home from a weekend seminar some years ago, my wife, Marilyn, and I were discussing impressions of the people we had met. The seminar involved several small groups and she and I had not been in the same group. I asked her if she had had a chance to meet George somebody-or-other—I couldn't even remember his last name—a fellow who had been in the same group as I. She said she had.

"What did you think?" I asked.

"Oh . . ." she hesitated.

"Well, he just about drove me nuts," I said. She wondered why. "I don't know," I said, "but he really got on my nerves."

Then she laughed and said, "He is an intelligent person, but he likes to talk a lot, and pretty well monopolizes the conversation in the group."

"Yes," I said. "So? . . ."

"Well," she said, "you have a tendency to do the same thing yourself. That's probably why you can't stand him."

A nation's defense system is built on the volume and sophistication of weaponry amassed, readiness to activate the system, and early warning of the necessity to activate. It is essentially the same with individuals—that is where we learned it. I was under attack. The enemy was right next to me in the car seat. Alarms sounded, red lights flashed, and my computer printed out: Activate defense! She had barely finished her sentence and the words were in my throat. All systems were "go." Heart rate increased, respiration up, blood thickening, stomach clamping shut, etc. Ready to fire. Fire one!

"Alright," I said, "just what do you mean by *that*!"

Two centuries ago Robert Burns wrote:

> O wad some Pow'r the giftie gie us
> To see oursels as others see us!
> It wad frae mony a blunder free us,
> And foolish notion.

Critics can do us a lot of favors if we can only talk down our narcissism which wants to cry out every time we are "wounded" in an "attack" by those who would hold up our weaknesses for us to look at. Of course criticism is often painful —a person would *much* rather receive positive, complimentary feedback. So we can avoid the pain by silencing the critic either through refutation with competitive power or through subtle manipulation. Whatever, every time we choose to react in this way we lose an opportunity for the possible new awareness that the critic, whether friendly or hostile, may well be offering.

As I mentioned in Chapter 4, theological students and professional clergy often come into a program of clinical pastoral education declaring the vague goal of wanting to grow. Elaborated this usually means developing skills in the doing of ministry in a clinical or critical setting as well as increased self-awareness and self-understanding.

Though students are quite sincere in declaring the latter to be a hoped-for expectation, it is often a different story once the opportunity for it presents itself. Increased self-awareness does not come readily from a book; it offers itself through human interaction with peers, staff, and supervisor. And a student will gain it only to the degree that he or she is willing to suffer a view of the shadow.

The person wishing to discover his shadow will want to test out feedback which identifies shadow qualities which have been surfaced. If I had inquired among friends and colleagues about how my behavior appeared to them in small groups and not one of them agreed with Marilyn's assessment, then in all probability her observation would be inaccurate and would be coming from some other dynamic (it would be "her problem," so to speak). But if a half dozen assorted persons from time to time directly or indirectly (and most of the time it *is* indirectly) let me know that I talk a lot in small groups and tend to monopolize the conversation, then I would do well to believe that there is truth in

Marilyn's observation and I am indeed looking into the face of my dark side. I can no longer go blithely wandering into a small group, ready to "chat away," naively believing that the people in the group are just waiting for me to come in and take over the conversation. My ego will wince at that, but I will have moved ever so slightly forward in my journey towards wholeness.

Let me say here by way of illustration, it would be possible for me to slip into despondency over this insight—this view of my shadow. It would be possible for me to review my life and assess how many people I had offended; how insensitive, even rude, I must have been; how egocentric; how often people must have tolerated me to my face and behind my back said, "Good grief, what a bore." Here my traveling companion can help me quite substantially in reevaluating my self-image in light of my total personality rather than establishing it on the basis of one observation of my shadow side. He will not discount my sincere sorrow over past behavior, but will be able to help me celebrate the fact that I no longer need to perform this behavior because I "know better." *Doing it* (that is, restraining my urge to monopolize the conversation) will be something else—that is the matter of control, that is to "suffer" my shadow, because the next time the opportunity presents itself I will still want to monopolize the conversation; the shadow does not die. But my new awareness (consciousness) will allow me the opportunity to use constructively in the small group what prior to my awareness I used egocentrically.

Have you ever caught yourself saying or doing something contrary to what you intended to say or do or what you usually say or do? If so, you have experienced another valid and common way of becoming acquainted with your shadow side. Slips of the tongue are often humorous, sometimes embarrassing, and occasionally downright disastrous. Suppose you invite a female friend to your party, not because you want to but because you feel a social and moral obligation. You would rather not invite her because she is quite tedious and artificial and is known to "get on people's nerves." Consequently you are delighted (internally, of course) when you phone her to invite her and she tells you that she will be "tickled pink" to attend, but will "unfortunately" have to leave early for another engagement.

On the night of the party she is present, tedium and all, and about midway into the evening she approaches you in the midst of your conversation with friends, and says, "Oh, darling, thank you so very much for such a lovely party, but I really must be going." And with ever so slight an expression of sad pain on your face you reply, "Do you *have* to stay? Can't you go?"

I once heard a young woman introduce a high school choral group as they were about to present a Christmas concert in our church auditorium. The group processed in and took their places on the risers. The young woman stood up and announced, "Ladies and gentlemen, I'd like to introduce to you the West High School Choral Group who will now present a program of sacred and sexual music."

Anytime you experience such a slip, gaffe, *faux pas,* blooper, typo, whatever you choose to call it, you can be relatively sure that your shadow has brushed by and you would do well to look at it. You may declare, "That is the absolute *last* thing I wanted to say; my brain played a trick on me." Perhaps. But perhaps also that was the absolute *first* thing your shadow wanted to say and *it* was the trickster.

Slips of behavior are not unlike slips of tongue; they, too, can help us get to know our shadow. Again there is probably not one among us who has never said, "I don't know what came over me!" or "I wasn't myself!" or "It was like a dream!" or "I just had no control!" or "I never do that." When your action is contrary to your intended behavior, your shadow side has called the shot. That is distressing enough, but we are not always even aware of this happening. For example, if you are driving home from a party and your spouse says to you, "Whatever got into you tonight?" and you honestly don't know what he or she is referring to, be prepared to meet your shadow, because your spouse is about to introduce you to it. If a friend or colleague tells you, "You haven't been acting like yourself," and you honestly are not aware of acting any differently than usual, don't ask him what he means unless you want to face your shadow.

Anytime you are perceived differently than you intended to be perceived, chances are you have been in the company of your shadow. If you are surprised to find that you have had a different effect on a person than you intended, your shadow has been manifested. People are sometimes shocked at the images others have of them when they learn them. "Where did you ever get *that* impression?" they ask with incredulity.

In these situations, where a slip of the tongue has occurred or where behavior was contrary to the person's persona or where the person produced an effect which he had no intention of producing or where he stumbled over some task which he expected he would perform easily and correctly, the speaker—the performer—has been not the conscious ego but the shadow. If you wish to become acquainted with your shadow, take the plunge and explore these phenomena in yourself. Otherwise you will simply continue to use phrases such as "Oh, how silly of me, I *never* do that" and "I simply wasn't myself" to keep yourself blind to what everyone else sees and to perpetuate your own delusion of living up to your standard of perfection.

If you choose to project your shadow then examine your projection and you will surely find your dark side. If, for instance, it seems as though everyone you are having dealings with is looking for a fight, ask yourself what *you* are so angry about. Your ego doesn't know, but your shadow does. Take a piece of paper and write down everything that is offensive to you in other people. Write in capital letters those things that are *particularly* offensive. Underline those particularly offensive characteristics that are simply despicable. Include everything in others that makes you angry and outraged; everything that you absolutely hate, loathe, despise, and abominate.

After completing such a list you will probably be rather worked up, but you have in all probability painted a fairly decent picture of your shadow. This would be especially true of those qualities which you capitalized and particularly true of those capitalized and underlined.

This exercise is accurate because of the ease with which we throw our evil and evil potential onto others and mistakenly believe we have gotten rid of it. Projection is an efficient mechanism because it succeeds in deception. It therefore requires substantial courage on the part of any human being to look at such a compilation as this list of attributes and be willing to own it as a representation of his shadow.

The converse of this proposition is equally accurate: the opposites of everything which I admire, respect, and envy in others help constitute my shadow. We have seen that if I despise Mr. X's greed, I can be sure that greed is real in my shadow. Likewise if I strongly admire Mr. Y's philanthropy, I can be sure that its opposite, greed, is real in my shadow. Furthermore, since the opposites of our persona qualities are constellated in our shadow, if I am socially charitable and generous I may be sure that greed is real in my shadow. In addition, the greater the intensity of the quality (i.e., generosity) in the persona, the greater the intensity of its opposite (i.e., greed) in the shadow.

Literature and drama provide countless characters with whom we can identify. Looking at who you identify with in novels, plays, movies, and television productions will give you insight into your shadow side. Is there anyone who has never rooted for the villain or secretly hoped the crook would get away with it? I remember reading once about a man who got so caught up in his identification with the "villain" of a stage play that he ran down the aisle of the theater, hurled himself up onto the apron of the stage, and attacked the "hero." He was arrested and fined.

Dreams, daydreams, and fantasies also present us with shadow material that can help us know our dark sides. Many people claim that they never daydream or fantasize, but again, this may only be their perception and not in fact the case. Does your mind not have any idle moments? What do you think about when there is nothing to think about? Where do your thoughts go when not directed by your consciousness? Granted, our society's preoccupation with activity and busyness does not cultivate "idle moments"; still, none of us is devoid of them. Look into them and you may discover shadow aspects.

Dreams may provide us with further encounter with the shadow. *Dreams: God's Forgotten Language* by John Sanford (Lippincott, 1968) and *God, Dreams and Revelation* by Morton Kelsey (Augsburg, 1974) are interesting books which may be helpful in understanding dreams.

When one's shadow appears in a dream it is a figure of the same sex as the dreamer, usually dark and sinister, perhaps a hunchback, a witch or wizard, not always clearly distinguishable. Sometimes he or she gives the impression of being criminal or outlawish. Often when a person has proceeded along the journey of becoming acquainted with the shadow it will appear as a figure which generates fright in the dreamer but which in some ways helps the dreamer in the dream.

After surveying this roster of ways of becoming acquainted with one's dark side, it should be profoundly clear that the task is no simple one. Still the desire for wholeness and completeness compels us to make the pilgrimage—to refuse to go on any longer unconscious of this vital part of ourselves, our shadow. In the encounter with the shadow, as we come face to face with it, we need to *yield* to the experience and be open to our insights. There is always the great temptation to resurrect all kinds of defenses so that we may technically and intelligently analyze the experience. But all that will do is successfully sidetrack the process, and protect us from "knowing" our dark counterpart; wholeness will always remain only something wished for, even longed for.

9

SHADOW
and wholeness

It is perhaps a truism, but things are not always what they appear to be. In fact, sometimes they turn out to be the precise opposite. For instance, that which appears to be or which one believes is *un*desirable may, upon examination, actually turn out to be very desirable indeed, and the person wonders why he didn't realize this long ago.

Such, I believe, is the case with our shadow. God knows that when we look into it we find plenty of evil there, but even evil *can be* used for good. As Joseph, patriarch of Israel, recounted his experience of being sold by his brothers, he said to them, "You meant evil against me; but God meant it for good" (Gen. 50:20).

But beyond evil itself we find in the shadow so *much* of personhood that is undeveloped or underdeveloped—diamonds in the rough, so to speak. The shadow contains more than unwanted evil tendencies; there are normal, healthy instincts that have never seen the light of day, realistic insights that may have emerged but were relegated back to the nether region for whatever reason, and creative impulses that may introduce a person to virtually a whole new experience of life. The shadow qualities are not necessarily obviously evil—they may be inferior, primitive, unadapted, awkward, childish. The shadow contains the qualities helpful in bringing the personality to wholeness, to completion. Those qualities may truly embellish and revitalize our lives and make them full—provided, of course, we have the courage to acknowledge and own them consciously.

I have one more story to tell which speaks directly to this whole matter. It is another tale from Zimmer's collection and is titled "The King and the Corpse." It is an ancient parable from India whose opening sequence describes the very essence of our problem. I retell the story from Zimmer's account.

Each day the king sat in state hearing petitions and dispensing justice. Each day a holy man, dressed in the robe of an ascetic beggar, approached the king and without a word offered him a piece of very ripe fruit. Each day the king accepted the "present" from the beggar and without a thought handed it to his treasurer who stood behind the throne. Each day the beggar, again without a word, withdrew and vanished into the crowd.

Year after year this precise same ritual occurred every day the king sat in office. Then one day, some 10 years after the holy man first appeared, something different happened. A tame monkey, having escaped from the women's apartments in the inner palace, came bounding into the hall and leaped up onto the arm of the king's throne. The ascetic beggar had just presented the king with his usual gift of fruit, but this time instead of passing it on to his treasurer as was his usual custom, the king handed it over to the monkey. When the animal bit into it, a precious jewel dropped out and fell to the floor.

The king was amazed and quickly turned to his treasurer behind him. "What has become of all the others?" he asked. But the treasurer had no answer. Over all the years he had simply thrown the unimpressive "gifts" through a small upper window in the treasure house, not even bothering to unlock the door. So he excused himself and ran quickly to the vault. He opened it and hurried to the area beneath the little window. There, on the floor, lay a mass of rotten fruit in various stages of decay. But amidst this garbage of many years lay a heap of precious gems.

Of course there is much more to this fascinating tale; this opening segment only serves to bring the king and the holy beggar together for the sake of the story which follows. But it is in this opening experience, magical though it be, that we are faced with a truth that we often tend to write off with a "Yes, but" kind of response; namely, things are *not* always what they appear to be, and that which appears to be or is believed to be undesirable may in fact be quite the opposite.

Day after day for 10 years the beggar approached the king and modestly offered his gift. Granted, it wasn't much of a gift —a piece of overripe fruit. Perhaps on occasion it was even beginning to spoil. But day after day the king "accepted" the offering only to reject it by quickly passing it on to his treasurer, giving the gift no further heed and the beggar no acknowledgment whatsoever. Indeed a word never passed between them in 10 years.

"Ah, but," you say, "how could he know?" Indeed! How can anyone ever *know?* Doesn't life itself, every morning, stand before every one of us, dressed in the very ordinary, perhaps even like a beggar, unannounced, unostentatious, and unexplained, just *there,* holding out its gift, its common offering? And do we not often fail to open the gift, or even to ask ourselves, "I wonder what *this* holds?" Perhaps we should at least break open the fruit and learn to separate the imperishable kernel from the part that has ripened only to fade and rot. But we permit the fruit, jewel and all, to be tossed away.

What is even more amazing than this is that the valuable, albeit common or even undesirable fruit is presented to us not only by the patient hand of outer life, *but particularly and especially from within our very own selves*. Everything the tale tells may be interpreted as simply ourselves and our lives. We accept with some indifference the fruit of our existence from without and *especially* from within, and we discover nothing particularly noteworthy about it. In fact, we may even consider it to be on occasion rather mushy, or even putrid. We take it and rather quickly hand it over to another of our "selves" who stands behind the throne.

For we are not one but many—a variety of personages. We like perhaps to give the impression, or even to believe ourselves, that we are only what we appear to be—the king on the throne. But we are, in fact, much more, and one of our other selves is the royal treasurer who has charge of the riches of our selves upon which we draw, on which we live, and by which we are either great or little monarchs. This royal treasurer appears in the tale to be no more concerned than the king about investigating the gifts, and likewise rejects them by disposing of them, throwing them carelessly into the dark chamber of the treasury. And there they lie, neglected and rotting; their beauty and value known to no one.

But there is still another "other"—a personage of ourselves—one which is quite different from the treasurer, and from all the other personages for that matter. One who is quite out of place in the kingly chambers. Our monkey! He belongs and regularly resides only in the inner courts of the palace where he can be attended by those who can keep an eye on him. But life being what it is and circumstances being what they are, things do get mixed up, and every now and again the monkey breaks loose and comes bounding out into public view and pokes his little monkey face into the king's business.

Unlike both the king and the king's treasurer, the monkey receives and accepts the beggar's fruit. The king is above it; the monkey is eager for it. He is uninhibited, playful, curious, and more often than not will "fool" with a thing until it is broken. So in true monkey fashion he exposes the jewel at the core of the fruit almost immediately. But it has no meaning for him, so he abandons it and shuffles off to satisfy another curiosity or enjoy another fun.

All this is perhaps well and good you say, but in pragmatic terms what really is "in it" for the person willing to take the risk and pay the price and bite into the overripe fruit? What do these gems look like?

The first thing we discover is that we would do well to expand our insight about our lightness and darkness into much *more* of our experience of life. In coming to terms with our shadow we learn that we are indeed not all we appear to be. We may discover a need to rethink our attitudes and review our values. That, too, may be easier said than done; if I am unwilling to confess to myself that I may very well have been wrong all these years thinking or believing such and such was right (or wrong), I will probably be too rigid to modify or change my position and will consequently remain on dead center. I may have a vague notion or even an intellectual awareness that what I have believed to be undesirable, wrong, or even evil all these years may *not* after all be all that undesirable, wrong, or evil; *but* believing and acting on that new insight, moving beyond a mere intellectual nod, may prove to be too threatening to my ego foundation and demanding of more change than I frankly have the courage to make. Unless I take hold of myself and shake the pillars of my rigidity which so nicely protect my security, I will remain precisely where I am: secure in my familiar position, but troubled in my innermost self with vague but chronic dissatisfaction and unfulfillment and longings for something "more."

Most boys go through the growing-up process believing in the macho image of masculinity. That was certainly my experience, and while I was definitely not devoid of the attributes of tenderness, patience, and compassion, they were certainly subordinate to my assertive, even aggressive, self. As I continued to grow up, and through the years of my professional training, my feminine self emerged from the shadow and allowed me the experience of a more whole (balanced, integrated) posture. I experienced this fulfillment clearly in my role as pastoral counselor because I allowed it to develop there; however, in my role as teacher I apparently chose to disallow the development, believing, I suppose, that I needed to be strong and assertive, consistently pressing my students on in their learning and their performance. Whatever, I remember vividly the struggle of those days, not really being conscious of what was lacking; knowing that something *was* missing, but nevertheless denying the *anima* (my feminine counterpart) in my teacher role. My colleagues offered insight and feedback, but I successfully tuned that out because obviously it was not what I wanted to hear or had any intention of acting on.

One night I had a simple dream. I was in a room with peers and students. Although I could not see them in the dream I was aware that they were present. I was stripped to my waist, and I was struggling to put on a woman's brassiere. I had it on, straps over shoulder, but was wriggling around in it trying to get comfortable. I said, "This doesn't quite fit yet." And that was the end of the dream.

To *me* the dream was a milestone. To *me* the brassiere was a

132

clear symbol of femininity. I was into it, that was clear; but it wasn't comfortable. Not yet. The beauty of this message resided in the word *yet,* because the implication was that it would—it would ultimately fit. I *could* lay aside that strong-willed, assertive persona, and I *could* let in my tender, patient, compassionate feminine self, and I *would* feel comfortable with it. Now I knew, but I still had to act. I still had to let it be. And I did.

I had rejected much of the *anima,* the feminine counterpart of my macho-type persona. While I obviously did not see that part of me as being evil or undesirable, I certainly saw it as being subordinate. And conversely, while I did not necessarily see the machismo as righteous or the greatest good, I certainly saw it as being preferable. Then in my dream I experienced a revelation, and afterward I said to myself, "I was wrong. What I thought was superior wasn't. What I thought was inferior wasn't. I was wrong." So I began the process of change. I did not abandon my assertiveness and ego-strength. Nor did I become my *anima.* I began a tempering of both into a unification which has continued and which will continue. And I perceive this to be a significant movement toward wholeness and completeness.

This is not at all an unusual experience in becoming acquainted with the shadow. As we become conscious of our dark side we also become more aware of our light. When we perceive them thus simultaneously we have an opportunity to disengage ourselves from both and we are free to take a stand in the middle. We can learn to disidentify with our virtues as well as our vices because it becomes clear that neither is purely one nor the other.

Samuel Butler wrote in *The Way of All Flesh,*

People divide off vice and virtue as though they were two

things, neither of which had anything of the other. This is not so. There is no useful virtue which has not some alloy of vice, and hardly any vice, if any, which carries not with it a little dash of virtue; virtue and vice are life and death . . . things which cannot exist without being qualified by their opposites.

Can vice be virtue and virtue vice?
Just as nice be naughty and naughty nice!

Steven Swanson, in his book *The Double Cross* (Augsburg, 1980), helps us to see how our time-honored virtues can be deadly. Martin Luther, in his comments on Romans 6:14, identifies potential good in seeming evil. For example, an awareness of arrogance in the shadow puts humility in the ego into focus too. One may thus see good and evil in both and disengage himself from both to take a new stand somewhere in the middle —somewhere in the unification of the opposites. Thus arrogance, while considered an undesirable quality, can indeed be used constructively when brought into consciousness; it can temper humility which in itself has the potential of abuse in its extreme. This is simply the previous observation all over again, that "Too much morality is as bad as too little morality."

Likewise the uncovering of the trait of sloth or laziness (which is generally considered undesirable) in the shadow can provide a tempering of compulsivity and the obsession with performance. The undesirable characteristics of avarice and covetousness may be used positively as righteous ambition. Rendering unconscious envy conscious allows a person to acknowledge good in others—to credit others with what he had previously been trying to deny others or, in fact, steal from them.

Sloppiness may temper fastidiousness. Earthiness may temper prudishness. Playfulness may temper compulsivity. Relaxation may temper control. Egocentricity and selfishness may be tempered into appropriate assertiveness. Acceptance of sinfulness makes grace all the more precious.

In the process of making friends with the shadow we continually discover "good" in the shadow's "evil"—that the undesirable may indeed be used constructively, that the negative may be used positively. Correspondingly we discover that the ego itself was by no means so wholly "good" as we might have supposed—that there may be substantial superficiality and artificiality embodied in the persona. And these insights make integration possible. There is no capitulation to or identification with evil when we make friends with the shadow—what happens is that *we actually overcome evil with good.* Only the good is now our good which has been brought about through the agonies and the ecstasies of pilgrimage toward wholeness.

It would appear that the better we know and understand ourselves the more we can be in control of ourselves and our destinies and the less we will be controlled by our unconscious selves. We may jest about and make light of our experiences of shadow breakthrough, but simply saying, "I don't know what came over me; I just wasn't myself" will not correct or repair the damages of an uncontrolled spurt of shadow acting-out. We *need* to recognize and admit to the potential in ourselves for the commission of great evil. We need to own that potential as ours, not as belonging only to "them," or "him," or "her," or "it." We need to say to our shadow, "Yes, my shadow, I acknowledge you and your power as part of me, and I respect the magnitude of that power. But I will not forget, nor will you, shadow, that *the power of light is greater than the power of darkness.*"

Ignorance is an enemy. The perpetuation of ignorance by the refusal of growth in self-awareness may be comfortable, but it provides a false sense of security and makes a person most vulnerable. Being ignorant of our true selves means that we only continue blindly along, assuming that our well-meaning conscious personality expresses the truth of what we really are. This quite effectively eliminates any possibility of moral and spiritual growth.

It is so simple to deceive ourselves with our own goodness and in that deception be swept into the very things we would most avoid. Thomas à Becket in T. S. Eliot's play *Murder in the Cathedral* presents us with one of the finest expressions of moral insight and honest self-awareness. As Archbishop Thomas sits on the cathedral steps waiting for the men whom he knows will come to kill him because of his opposition to the king, he says, "But what is there to do? What is left to be done? Is there no enduring crown to be won?" And a tempter replies, "Yes, Thomas, yes . . . seek the way of martyrdom, make yourself the lowest on earth, to be high in heaven." Finally Thomas concludes:

> "Now is my way clear, now is the meaning plain:
> Temptation shall not come in this kind again.
> The last temptation is the greatest treason:
> To do the right deed for the wrong reason."

So a second benefit of making friends with our shadow is the increase in self-awareness that allows us to be more in the driver's seat of our lives and less controlled by our unconscious. For example, when we see violence in ourselves we can wrestle with it to overcome it. If we refuse to see it, the potential of being overcome by it is substantially greater—we don't even know what is happening in us. Jung repeatedly encouraged people to keep their conscious ego close to their shadow so they could keep their eye on it and not lose sight of it. I once heard of an Indian tribe in the Southwest who always invite Coyote, their equivalent of Satan, to their tribal council's powwow and provide a place for him. Their idea, of course, is that if he is there they can keep an eye on him, whereas if he's out of sight there is no telling what he might do.

The more deeply we know ourselves, the more authentic we may be as human beings; our personas don't have to be as thick or as varied. This is another substantial benefit of making friends with our shadow. We become better able to accept our humanity and to lay aside some of the unreasonable expectations we cherish for superhumanity.

Without a shadow you are unreal, you are unnatural. It means you have no substance, no reality—you cannot impress on real objects which have substance. There is a medieval legend about a man who sold his shadow to the devil. (According to superstition only the devil has no shadow and that is because he is allegedly *all* evil.) He sold it for quite a sum and was very pleased with the bargain. He set out to enjoy his newly won wealth, but encountered troubles immediately. Friends, acquaintances, and even strangers drew back from him when they noticed that he cast no shadow. "You have no substance," they said. "You are not a human being. You must be an incarnated spirit with some evil intent." And they ran away.

Everybody fled him because of his "unreality" and soon the isolation became more than he could bear. He sought out the devil and demanded that he return his shadow. But the devil only laughed.

In actual life something of the same thing happens. Though we generally prize high morals and good behavior, we believe there is something wrong if life is not "spiced" by something other than that. If we see no shadow, no hint that there is something more in this person than his unreproachable exterior, we begin to feel a little twitchy and tend to back away wondering where his "badness" is. Will it sneak out and "do us in" from whence we least expect it? Or is he truly superhuman?

These "innocents" are all around us—people whose righteousness encapsulates them and generates in people who observe them a variety of feelings ranging from respect through fear to rage. Rollo May, in his book *Power and Innocence* (W. W. Norton & Co., Inc.), wonders if through innocence one can incite being victimized. Does such a person's own shadow actually lead him into becoming a victim? These are indeed interesting questions.

I don't think it has ever been difficult for most Christians to accept that God endowed us with a free will knowing full well that he ran the risk of our using that freedom to exist contrary to rather than in harmony with his will. Without this endowment we would, of course, be mere robots or puppets—creatures who could do nothing but coincide our wills with God's will. We could not, then, be moral creatures. This endowment by God was therefore a very wise although risky move, because if a person does not have the capacity to hate, of what real value or significance is his love? Is not, in fact, the possibility of an opposing will a necessary condition for actualizing wholeness and completeness?

But whereas it has not been difficult for most Christians to accept that God endowed us with a free will, I believe it has been substantially difficult, if not impossible, for many Christian people to accept what it means in actual experience. It means our shadow is real. For if our shadow is not real, we are incapable of moral decision. And this is what is frightening. It would seem to indicate that those people who tell me that under no circumstance whatsoever could they willfully destroy the life of a human being—those people may be incapable of moral decision!

The technologization of our society in the Western world has given us an existence that is beyond what were even the wildest fantasies of most of our ancestors. Generally speaking, though, the majority of us would agree that we have paid a rather hefty price to acquire it, though not too many would be willing to abandon it. The single most important part of that price (which I believe escapes much of our awareness) is the fact that technologization has taken us away from the earth—it has removed us from the primitive. We are in danger of losing our earthiness of the earth and our saltiness of the sea. And these give us substance.

It is sadly strange that many righteous people classify earthiness and saltiness as undesirable traits. An "earthy" person is to some the precise opposite of a spiritually minded person. And a "salty" character is one of even lesser caliber in the judgment of the righteous.

Making friends with your shadow will be sure to get you in touch with your earthiness and saltiness. It will put your feet on the ground and take your head out of the clouds. It will orient you to reality and make you a solid person. It will put you in touch with your natural and primitive side, as well as your body, and help you along the way to wholeness.

Making friends with your shadow helps facilitate your acceptance of yourself as a less-than-perfect human being. We have a dark side; we are not all light. Of course I am a decent person, but I am sometimes a louse. Of course I am generous, but I am also greedy. The more I love, the more I can hate. I sacrifice, but I am selfish. I trust, but I also doubt. I am honest, yet I can be a crook. I am naive, but I am cunning. I succeed and I fail. I create and I destroy. I am angelic and I am demonic. I am faithful and I am a traitor.

Is this to boast? God forbid! I abhor my evil. It is disgusting and saddening. I stand guilty. But still, in the darkness of my shadow, I stand in the light of God's grace. I abandon my Pharisaic expectations and accept reality. I will surrender my mountaintop ideals and my hope for moral perfection—that goal will be replaced by the goal of endeavoring not to take myself too seriously. Perfectability may be technologically achievable, but not in the case of ethics or moral behavior.

The more we are able to accept ourselves as we are, the less we need to pretend to be something we aren't. This allows us to feel more secure within ourselves and in our relationships with others. I can be more transparent and not be so threatened by what you might think of me. In my transparency you may see more of the real me and less of the front that I otherwise must keep up but which blocks penetrating and deep relationships with human beings. The acknowledgment of imperfection is needed to build relationships with others.

This brings us into still another benefit of making friends with our shadow. The more I can accept myself in my imperfection the more I become able to accept others in their imperfection. I can cease projecting, and others are relieved of the burden of carrying my shadow. "I am always right in matters such as this; you must be wrong," will become "I am sometimes mistaken; you may very well be right."

To say that and to believe it is to realize again how much courage is required in this process of moving toward wholeness. "It was my fault," "I made the mistake," "I did it," and similar phrases which own our responsibility for our being and our actions—these phrases stick in our throats and almost make us gag when we hold to the image of faultlessness. To throw the responsibility or the blame onto the other person is *so* simple. But he who will own his own shadow qualities will no longer direct his anger and resistance towards the other person who seems to embody those qualities, but will instead use the energy to modify or eliminate them in himself.

The process of moving towards wholeness and completeness *(teleios)* is the process of life; it does not cease throughout our experience of this life. We move forward and we regress. We experience peace and we experience conflict. Heightened awareness and heightened sense of responsibility make the task a real moral challenge. Values become modified or changed or reinforced, but they become in the process *our own* rather than inherited or naively or blindly accepted values. We see the variation between what we consciously hold as morality and what we unconsciously hold. We wrestle now with evil in ourselves instead of blithely suppressing or unknowingly repressing it. We accept our irrationality and our instinct as we accept our rationality and our reason. We exercise self-control and discipline, for the bit in the mouth is being replaced by the reins in the hand.

But once you are in the saddle, you must choose; mere awareness of the moral conflict is not enough, you must act. Of course you can always renounce one side in favor of the other, or you can beat a retreat from the conflict altogether, or you can struggle for the seemingly impossible solution that will satisfy both sides.

How can such seemingly contradictory opposites as good and evil be reconciled? Only by transcending them; by raising the issue to a higher level wherein the contradiction may be resolved.

When I am able successfully to detach myself from identifying with either opposite, I am often surprised at how nature or the activity of the divine in natural process can intervene to help me. This very much depends on my attitude. The more open and receptive I can be, keeping myself as free as I can from hard and fast principles, and the more I am willing honestly to let go of my ego-will (what I want), the better are my chances of being "grabbed" by something greater than my thoughts or my reason or my will that will bring out in my experience the resolution of the conflict.

This transcendence of good and evil was, I believe, best illustrated by Jesus in Gethsemane. The touchstone of this experience is the sacrifice of will to the will of God, and as we all know, we dearly love to resist doing that. But when it occurs, when we allow ourselves to let it be, a transformation takes place in good and evil; good seems to lose some of its good and evil seems to lose some of its evil. And the solution is neither good nor evil, but is *right* for us.

Only he who is substantially conscious of the light should journey into his darkness. For the darkness will convict him and seek to destroy him and only the light can save him. Therefore we seek more light, more goodness, more moral strength and stamina as we make friends with our shadow. For that we *must do* no matter what.

> Nevertheless in this dark conscience it behooveth thee to labour and sweat; and then when thou findest right nought but sorrow and pain and blindness in this darkness, if thou wilt find Jhesu thou must suffer the pain of this dark conscience and abide awhile therein. For within this nought is Jhesu hid in his joy, whom thou shalt not find with all thy seeking unless thou pass this darkness.

> *In him was life,*
> *and the life was the light of men.*
> *The light shines in the darkness,*
> *and the darkness has not overcome it.*

> (John 1:4-5)